Nimrod MRA4

Demise of the Mighty Hunter

Hugh Harkins

Copyright © 2021 Hugh Harkins FRAS, MIstP, MRAeS

All rights reserved.

ISBN: 1-903630-43-6
ISBN-13: 978-1-903630-43-3

Nimrod MRA4

© 2021 Hugh Harkins FRAS, MIstP, MRAeS

Centurion Publishing

United Kingdom

ISBN 10: 1-903630-43-6
ISBN 13: 978-1-903630-43-3

This volume first published in 2021

The author is identified as the copyright holder of this work under sections 77 and 78 of the Copyright Designs and Patents Act 1988

Cover design © Centurion Publishing & KDP

Page layout, concept and design © Centurion Publishing

All rights reserved. No part of this publication may be reproduced, stored in a retrieval system, transmitted in any form, or by any means, electronic, mechanical or photocopied, recorded or otherwise, without the written permission of the publisher

This volume has adopted a quasi-Harvard Manual of Style for referencing. It has, however, not always been possible to adopt a standard referencing format

CONTENTS

	Introduction	vii
1	Nimrod MRA4 Lineage	1
2	Nimrod MRA4	13
3	Development and Test to Cancellation	59
4	Postscript	87
5	Glossary	88
6	Bibliography	90

INTRODUCTION

The Nimrod MRA4 was an ambitious program intended to provide the British Royal Air Force with a high capability multi-mission aircraft with an emphasis on anti-submarine warfare/anti-surface strike/maritime patrol missions. As the focus of the volume is the Nimrod MRA4 program, only a brief resume of the design heritage going back to the first and second generation Nimrod, themselves derived from the de Havilland DH106 Comet 4, is provided.

The volume draws on textual and graphic material from the respective design house/test team and governmental papers in an attempt to arrive at an objective account of the program from inception, development/testing, to cancellation, almost on the eve of service entry.

1

NIMROD MRA4 LINEAGE

From the end of the Second World War until the cancellation of the Nimrod MRA4 program in October 2010, the United Kingdom of Great Britain and Northern Ireland had maintained a land based long-range maritime patrol/anti-submarine aircraft fleet. This had been done through service of converted Avro Lancaster piston engine bombers then the purpose designed Avro Shackleton, (developed from the Avro Manchester/Lancaster/Lincoln lineage), which was superseded by the jet powered Hawker Siddeley (later British Aerospace) Nimrod MR1 from the late 1960's, and the Nimrod MR2, which became operational in the late 1970's and served into the second decade of the twenty first century.

Hawker Siddeley had commenced work on their HS801 project at Woodford in June 1964 – the origins of the Nimrod design could be traced back to the de Havilland Comet, the first Jet powered airliner. The Nimrod MR1 was designed and received certification under Ministry of Defence specification MR 254 D&P, which was released in 1965. This governed that the Comet 4C design, which formed the basis of the Nimrod MR1 design, was certified under British Civil aviation Airworthiness Requirements in force from 1956 (NR, 2009).

Two Comet 4C aircraft were allocated for conversion as HS801 (formally named Nimrod in 1967) development aircraft. Converting the Comet 4C to Nimrod MR1 standard involved significant changes to the fuselage, the length of which was reduced by ~1.98 m (~78 in). Although the Comet circular section fuselage was retained, a large unpressurised lower fuselage section was added to accommodate a stores bay and radar antenna, giving the aircraft what could be termed a double circular cross section. The vertical tail fin was modified and a Magnetic Anomaly Detector, housed in an elongated boom, was located in the extreme rear fuselage. A powerful searchlight (~70 million candle power illumination) for the search and rescue role was housed in the forward section of the starboard wing fuel tank. The undercarriage system, consisting of two eight wheel main units and a twin steerable nose wheel unit, was similar to that fitted to the Comet 4C.

The Nimrod MRA4 (PA02 illustrated) was the last of the line of Nimrod variants evolving over the course of more than four decades. BAE Systems

The conversion process included replacing the four Avon turbojet engines of the Comet 4C with four Rolls Royce Spey 250 (RB.168) engines. In order to extend operational range the Nimrod MR1 was to be capable of shutting down up to two engines during a patrol and restarting them when required for normal cruise flight. This necessitated the installation of an integral air starter system in the Spey 250 and installation of an integral APU (Auxiliary Power Unit), which was installed in the Nimrod MR1 tail section, as well as installation of a duct complex. This allowed hot air to be routed from the APU to the starter turbine in the Spey engine to re-start engine(s) in-flight – a cross-feed duct allowed hot pressurised air to be passed from the engine(s) on the port side to engine(s) on the starboard side and vice versa (NR, 2009).

The Comet 4 (top), from which the HS810 Nimrod was derived, could trace its design lineage to the original de Havilland Comet 1 (above), which flew on 27 July 1949. BAE Systems

Two additional fuel tanks, No.5 and No.6, were installed under the cabin in the fuselage of the Nimrod MR1 (these areas were converted from the baggage/cargo compartment in the Comet 4C) and a further two, No.7 (port) and No.7 (starboard), on the fuselage sides contained within the area of the wing root (NR, 2009).

Top: The Nimrod MR1 ASV-21 radar was carried over from the Shackleton MR3 (illustrated). Centre: Following conversion from Comet 4 C standard, the first prototype Nimrod MR1, XV148, conducted its post conversion maiden flight in May 1967. The aircraft is shown minus the extended tail boom that would house the magnetic anomaly detector sensor, a distinctive feature off the MR1, MR and the MRA4. Bottom: The second Nimrod MR1 prototype, XV247, during a development flight. BAE Systems

Top: Nimrod MR1 XV245. Bottom: Nimrod MR1 XV236 at upper altitude in summer 1979. Crown Copyright/BAE Systems

The prototype Nimrod MR1, XV148, converted from Comet 4C standard, conducted its post conversion maiden flight on 23 May 1967. The second prototype, XV147, flew on 31 July 1967 – this was the only Nimrod to be powered by four Rolls Royce Avon turbojet engines as the Spey was selected for serial produced Nimrod aircraft.

RAF Nimrod MR1 XV231 on the ramp at naval air station Norfolk, Virginia, USA, on 17 January 1984. US DoD

A total of 38 Nimrod MR MK1 aircraft were ordered for the RAF (Royal Air Force) in early 1965, with the first serial production example conducting its maiden flight from Woodford on 28 June 1968. On 2 October the following year, deliveries commenced to the MOTU (Maritime Operational Training Unit) – this was later renamed No.236 OCU (Operational Conversion Unit) – based at RAF St. Mawgan, Cornwall. Five RAF squadrons were subsequently equipped with Nimrod MR1, two at St Mawgan and three at RAF Kinloss in Northern Scotland. Deliveries to Kinloss had commenced with the thirteenth serial aircraft on 25 June 1970, beginning the re-equipment process for No.120, 201 and 206 squadrons. No.203 Squadron, based at Luqa, Malta, was the last unit to equip with Nimrod MR1, the first example arriving on 31 July 1971. The RAF received the last of the initial 38 production Nimrod MR1 on 18 September 1972, although continued production was assured with the January 1972 announcement that a further eight airframes were required as spare and attrition replacements. These aircraft were formally ordered in 1974, with the first flying in November that year. The British withdrawal from Malta, in 1979, had reduced the number of Nimrod airframes required by the RAF, therefore, three were retained at Woodford for experimental work, two of which were subsequently converted to Spey 251 powered Nimrod AEW (Airborne Early Warning) MK3 standard. The remaining five aircraft were delivered as planned to the RAF.

Initially several surplus Nimrod MR1 airframes were converted to Nimrod R1 electronic reconnaissance standard. USN

In the mid-1970's, a sensor update was mooted for the Nimrod MR1 fleet, which would ultimately lead to the Nimrod MR MK2. Installation of more powerful sensors resulted in the generation of increased temperatures, necessitating installation of a supplementary conditioning pack in the aircraft rear section. Design and certification of the Nimrod MR2 was accomplished under specification MR 286 D&P of 6 May 1975 (NR, 2009). On 23 June the following year, the Nimrod prototype, XV148, flew with new avionics/sensors installed. This was followed by three trial conversion Nimrod MR1s, which flew post conversion in March 1978, May 1978 and March 1979 respectively. The last of these development aircraft actually followed the first production conversion, which flew as a Nimrod MR2 on 13 February 1979 and entered service with No.201 Squadron at RAF Kinloss on 23 August that year. The Kinloss Nimrod Wing was the first to re-equip with the MR2, relinquishing its last Nimrod MR1 in October 1982. Conversion of 32 Nimrod MR1 to Nimrod MR2 standard was completed in 1985.

A Nimrod MR2 cycles the cavernous stores bay doors during a flight over RAF Leuchars, Scotland. Author

The conversion of Nimrod MR1 to Nimrod MR2 standard changed the appearance and, fundamentality, the operational capability of the Nimrod fleet. External changes included deletion of a cabin window, modified air intakes to increase feed efficiency for the engines, and ducts around the rear fuselage, along with the repositioning of some of the external antenna/aerials. The main leap forward in capability concerned the mission systems, with the replacement of the outdated early Nimrod MR1's ASV-21 radar (handed down from the Avro Shackleton MR3 maritime patrol/anti-submarine warfare aircraft) with the then modern

Thorn EMI ARI 5980 Searchwater radar. This radar, featuring around fifty times the processing performance of the ASV-21, was designed to detect and classify small targets against the clutter of heavy seas. The identification friend or foe complex was integrated into the Searchwater, which was endowed with weather, navigation and search modes. The Searchwater system also featured an extensive track while scan capability, with multiple targets being tracked and classified simultaneously. For the primary anti-submarine warfare mission the Nimrod MR2 was equipped with a GEC Avionics AQS 901 acoustic processor.

Initial weapons employed by the Nimrod MR2 fleet included the BAe Dynamics (Matra British Aerospace Dynamics Alenia) MK11 depth charge, which had a maximum operating depth of 90 m (~295 ft.), along with the MK44, as initially employed on the Nimrod MR1. In addition, the Nimrod was apparently cleared to carry the United States B57 nuclear depth bomb, which had a yield of between five and ten kilotons, and an operating depth of around 1000 m (~3,281 ft.). In the post-Cold War period, the RAF relinquished the nuclear armed role and all nuclear free fall bomb/depth charges were retired.

In early 1977, a Nimrod at RAF Kinloss had an experimental camouflage scheme of a brownish grey colour, officially known as Hemp, applied. This was later adopted by the operational fleet, including the Nimrod R MK1 ELINT (Electronic Intelligence) aircraft (powered by the Spey 251) and the Nimrod AEW3 (later cancelled) between 1980 and 1982. It was the requirements for long-rang operations during the Falklands War of 1982 that led to the introduction of a temporary inflight refueling capability for the Nimrod MR2 – aircraft so modified were often referred to as Nimrod MR2P. This was later modified, in line with formal requirements for the Nimrod AEW3 and incorporated as a formal design of the entire Nimrod fleet, which would be carried over to the Nimrod MRA4.

By 1996, when the Nimrod 2000 was selected to succeed the Nimrod MR2, Nimrods had served the RAF in MR1, MR2 (maritime reconnaissance) and R1 (electronic reconnaissance/intelligence gathering) operations for several decades. The RAF Nimrod fleet had been extensively employed during the April-June 1982 Falklands War with Argentina in the South Atlantic, the 1991 Gulf War to remove Iraqi occupation forces from Kuwait, in the Balkans in the 1990's and the wars of occupation against Iraq and Afghanistan insurgents in the first decade of the twenty first century. In these latter conflicts the Nimrod MR2 moved from the primary surveillance/maritime patrol role to that of ELINT (Electronic Intelligence) gathering.

The Nimrod AEW MK3 was developed from the mid-1970's to superseded the elderly piston-engine Avro Shackleton AEW MK2. Nimrod AEW3 development aircraft XZ286 (top) and XV263 (bottom) were converted from surplus Nimrod MR1 airframes. These aircraft took on a distinctive appearance, with large bulbous extensions on the nose and tail sections to house the Marconi radar antennas. The AEW3 program was cancelled in 1983, and, along with it, plans to convert up to 11 Nimrod airframes to this standard. BAE Systems

BAE Systems Nimrod MR2

Type: Maritime reconnaissance aircraft
Power plant: 4 x Rolls Royce Spey 250 (RB.168) non-afterburner turbofan engines
Span without wingtip sensor pods: ~35.00 m (114 ft. 10 inch)
Length, with refuelling probe: ~39.34 m (129 ft. 1 inch)
Height: ~9.06 m (29 ft. 8.5 inch)
Wing area: ~197 m^2 (2,121 ft^2.)
Fuel: Internal, ~38936 kg (85,840 lb.); fuel fraction 0.48; in weapons bay displacing weapons, ~6849 kg (15,100 lb.)
Maximum speed: 926 km/h (500 knots/~575 mph)
Normal transit speed: ~787 km/h (425 knots/~489 mph);
Patrol speed on two engines: ~370 km/h (200 knots (~230 mph)
Ceiling: ~12802 m (42,000 ft.)
Ferry range on internal fuel without in-flight refuelling: ~9254 km (5,750 miles)
Unrefuelled combat radius: ~3706 km (2,000 nm (UK)/~2302 miles)
Patrol endurance: 12 hours unrefuelled
Armament: Up to ~6123 kg (13,500 lb.), including, sonobouys; AGM-84 anti-ship or AIM-9 air to air missile

Nimrod MR2P VX254 in January 1983 configured with the air to air armament of 4 x AIM-9 Sidewinder short range infrared guided missiles. BAE Systems

Nimrod MR2 from the Kinloss Wing at RAF Leuchars in the 1990's (top) and a Nimrod during night time flight line operations in the 2000's. Author/Crown Copyright

2

NIMROD MRA4

It is poignant that the cancellation of the Nimrod MRA4 (formerly Nimrod 2000) in 2010, with no apparent successor at the time of said cancellation, was progressed with, leaving the UK (United Kingdom of Great Britain and Northern Ireland) bereft of a long-range (long-endurance) airborne anti-submarine/maritime patrol capability, eroding the UK's ability to protect her independent nuclear deterrent. While it was true that the Nimrod MRA4 program had encountered significant delays to projected in-service date(s), the evidence would suggest that the cancellation was political/financial in nature, facilitating short term defence spending savings without due consideration of then present or projected future operational requirements. The Nimrod MRA4 program was cancelled more or less in concert with the retirement of the Nimrod MR2. This suggests, strongly, that the political decision had been taken that a fixed-wing, long-range maritime patrol/anti-submarine warfare capability was surplus to requirement. If this had not been the case then the logical position would have been to retain a small number of life-extant Nimrod MR2 until the delayed entry to service of the Nimrod MRA4 had been effected, or a replacement program sourced. It would not be illogical to arrive at the conclusion that the cancellation of the Nimrod MRA4 program, with no planned replacement, was among the most ill-considered defence planning decisions in modern history, perhaps on a par with that of Duncan Sandy's (Minster for Defence) infamous 1957 White Paper, which effectively cancelled several inhabited aircraft programs through the fallacy that military aviation in the post 1950's period would belong wholly to missiles.

The second of three Nimrod MRA4 development/prototypes, PA02, in flight over the Irish Sea. BAE Systems

It was clear in 2010, as it was in 2021, that the United Kingdom required to retain a high capability fixed-wing, long-range anti-submarine/maritime patrol capability. While the numerous media reports of Russian submarines operating in British waters in the post 2014 period are unsubstantiated, and most are outright preposterous in their assertion, it is clear that, given Britain had embarked upon a course of adversarial brinkmanship with the Russian Federation, it required a high capability anti-submarine platform to counter Russian advanced submarines, and, to a lesser degree, those of other nations. The advanced Russian submarines entering service in the second decade of the twenty first century – Project 636.2 (conventional powered attack/cruise missile submarine) (Harkins, 2016); Project 885/M (nuclear powered attack/cruise missile armed submarine) and Project 955/A (nuclear powered ballistic missile submarine – element of the Russian nuclear deterrent triad) (Harkins, 2019) – were designed, and ordered, in the years prior to and immediately following the cancellation of the Nimrod MRA4 program. More recently, the Russian Federation developed the Poseidon Oceanic Multipurpose System (uninhabited underwater nuclear warhead delivery system) as part her efforts to nullify NATO (North Atlantic Treaty Organisation) missile defence systems (Harkins,

2019). In the case of Poseidon, the operational characteristics of this system would render it difficult, even impossible (with current – 2020 technology levels), to counter in open ocean. However, it may be possible to counter such a vessel as it approached to and operated in littoral waters. Poseidon may be vulnerable whilst being deployed from its mothership – currently adaptions of the large Project 949A nuclear powered submarine (Harkins, 2019).

Nimrod MRA4 (Nimrod 2000) was considered an essential part of the defence of the UK independent nuclear deterrent through provisioning protection for Royal Navy Vanguard Class SSBN (nuclear powered, nuclear armed ballistic missile submarines) (page 15 top). Nimrod MRA4 would also have been tasked with protecting against threat submarines, including nuclear armed ballistic missile submarines (Project 955 SSBN of the Russian Federation Northern Fleet illustrated, circa 13 January 2019 (page 16)) and the nuclear armed Poseidon Oceanic Multipurpose System uninhabited underwater drone (page 15 bottom). BAE Systems/MODRF

The requirement that led to the Nimrod 2000 (later Nimrod MRA4) program was formulated in the early 1990's under the RMPA (Replacement Maritime Patrol Aircraft) program (RMPA remained the program name until 1999) (NAO, 1999), under the need to arrive at a design replacement for the Nimrod MR2 maritime patrol aircraft fleet. The intention was to arrive at a platform endowed with capability significantly in advance of that provided by the Nimrod MR2, which was approaching obsolescence, and to significantly enhance anti-surface warfare and intelligence gathering functionality of the maritime patrol fleet. Improved mission capability would be achieved through incorporation of, and integration between, advanced sensors and the modern human machine interface. Mission availability would be enhanced through advanced air platform technology and advancements in support infrastructure/maintenance (NOA, 2010).

In the late 1980's and into 1990, it was expected that the Lockheed P-7 evolution of the P-3 Orion (program cancelled in July 1990) would have been procured to meet the expectant RAF maritime patrol aircraft requirement to replace the Nimrod MR2. As depicted in this illustration, the P-7 offered expanded combat persistence potential through external carriage of up to twelve AGM-84 class air to surface missiles and carriage of anti-submarine warfare torpedoes in the internal stores bay. Lockheed Martin

In January 1992, the UK Ministry of Defence issued a draft ASR (Air Staff Requirement) – (ASR).420 was formalised in 1993 – which called for a Nimrod MR2 replacement with a projected 1998 in-service date. The RAF (Royal Air Force) had been expected to acquire a fleet of Lockheed (later Lockheed Martin) P-7 – evolution of the Lockheed P-3 Orion maritime patrol aircraft – four turboprop powered design under development in the late 1980's as a Lockheed P-3 Orion replacement for the USN (United States Navy), but this project was cancelled by the United States Department of Defence in July 1990. Following the P-7's demise, the designs available to fill the British requirement included updated Nimrod and the French Dassault Atlantic II (Atlantique 2), although this design had the disadvantage of having only two engines (the RAF preference was for a four engine aircraft to address over water safety concerns, although this was not set in stone). After cancellation of its P-7 Orion follow on, Lockheed offered updated P-3 designs, culminating in the Orion 2000. In the early 1990's, the Russian Beriev Be-42 was suggested as a potential contender, although this was more a case of speculative media hype than genuine consideration of the Russian type, which would have required an extensive redesign to accommodate western sourced systems and engines. This design had everything going against it, not least of which was the fact that, like the Atlantic II, it was a twin engine design. More importantly, the immediate post-Cold war political environment, although smooth by comparison of the 1980's, was unlikely to see Russian aircraft designs purchased for the RAF in any capacity.

Several Nimrod based options were proposed to meet ASR.420. These ranged from basic updates of the Nimrod MR2 (above) to comprehensive rebuilds that emerged as the Nimrod 2000. Author

The issue of Requests For Information was approved by the EAC (Equipment Approval Committee) in November 1992, with 17 companies/consortiums invited to submit proposals for the draft RMPA Staff Requirement. Analysis of the various responses led to an invitation to BAe (British Aerospace Ltd Military Aircraft Division – later BAE Systems), Lockheed, Loral and Dassault, to provide detailed technical and commercial proposals to meet the RMPA Staff Requirement. Following scrutiny by the EAC, four industry submissions from BAe, Lockheed Martin, Loral and Dassault Aviation, were invited to advance to the next phase. Each competitor was invited to submit detailed proposals, both technical and commercial, on their respective plans to arrive at a design capable of meeting the Staff Requirement (NAO MPR, 2010, PPR, 23.7.2003, NAO MPR, 2001 & NAO MPR, 1999).

To meet the **RMPA Staff Requirement, Dassault proposed a variation of its Atlantic II maritime patrol aircraft (top) while several P-3 update options were offered (bottom) from Lockheed and Loral – later both P-3 programs were administered through Lockheed Martin.** Dassault Aviation/USN

Dassault, which had forwarded a proposal for an advanced maritime patrol aircraft based on technologies matured in its twin turboprop powered Atlantic II maritime patrol/anti-submarine/surface strike aircraft, withdrew from the competition in January 1996. Lockheed and Loral merged in May that year (NAO MPR, 2001), the new entity of Lockheed Martin retaining the two proposals to meet the British Staff Requirement – the Orion 2000 proposal would have been equipped with the EL/2020 multi-mode radar complex and the EL/L-8300 Electronic Sensor Measures complex. This numerical advantage, in regard to numbers of advanced proposals, was to no avail, as, following intense scrutiny of all submissions, a BAe proposal, an advanced derivative of the tried and tested Nimrod design, was selected. The selection process had actually considered multiple Nimrod options before arriving at the Nimrod 2000 selection. The discarded options included a minimal cost update of the Nimrod MR2 and a non-updated run on of the extant Nimrod MR2 fleet (PPR, 23.7.2003), which would have extended service life, but added no capability enhancements required to counter projected threats over several decades of service.

British Aerospace proposed a comprehensive update of the Nimrod design, which would emerge as the Nimrod 2000 – an artist rendering showing retouching of the MR2 to Nimrod 2000 standard (illustrated) was released.
BAE Systems

Artist rendering depicting a Nimrod 2000 deploying a Sting Ray lightweight anti-submarine warfare torpedo over rough seas. BAE Systems

The Nimrod 2000 was selected to the meet the British Staff Requirement as it was the RMPA preferred option in regard to capability provision and industrial considerations (PPR, 23.7.2003 & NAO MPR, 1997). This proposal was to involve a refurbishment of most of the then extant Nimrod MR2 fleet – at the time of the preferred option selection (July 1996) there were 24 Nimrod MR2 in service with the Kinloss wing, while a further three were retained in storage. This would considerably extend the fatigue life of the newly emergent Nimrod 2000. The selected preferred option also included a re-engine program and installation of a modern avionics/sensor suite to meet performance and capability goals and reduced life cycle costs.

Following selection and approval by the EAC, the Nimrod 2000 was endorsed by government ministers on 25 July 1996 – equated to Main Gate approval (NAO MPR, 2010 & NAO MPR, 2001). In December 1996, the Nimrod RMPA ITP assumed reasonability for the program, which had previously lain with the PE (Procurement Executive (NR, 2009 & NAO MPR, 1997). The ~£2 billion fixed price contract covering the order for 21 mission capable Nimrod 2000 airframes, rebuilt from extant Nimrod MR2 airframes, along with associated training system and initial phase logistics, was formally awarded to prime contractor, BAe, in December 1996. The contract also covered provision of a suite of synthetic training equipment (aids), consisting of dynamic flight simulators for flight crew and training platforms for mission crew (NR, 2009 & NAO MPR, 1997).

Partnering the prime contractor, BAe, was several subcontractors – Rolls Royce/BMW (later Rolls Royce Germany) (engines) – FR (Flight Refuelling) Aviation (refurbishment of structures retained from the Nimrod MR2), Racal (Searchwater 2000MR radar complex), Boeing Defence & Aerospace Group (Tactical Command System and certain sensors) and Thomson Training and Simulation Ltd (Nimrod 2000 training aids) (NAO MPR, 1997). As prime contractor, BAe was responsible for overall management of the program, with design authority and responsibility for systems integration. This also included responsibility for platform qualification and release to service (BAE, 2002).

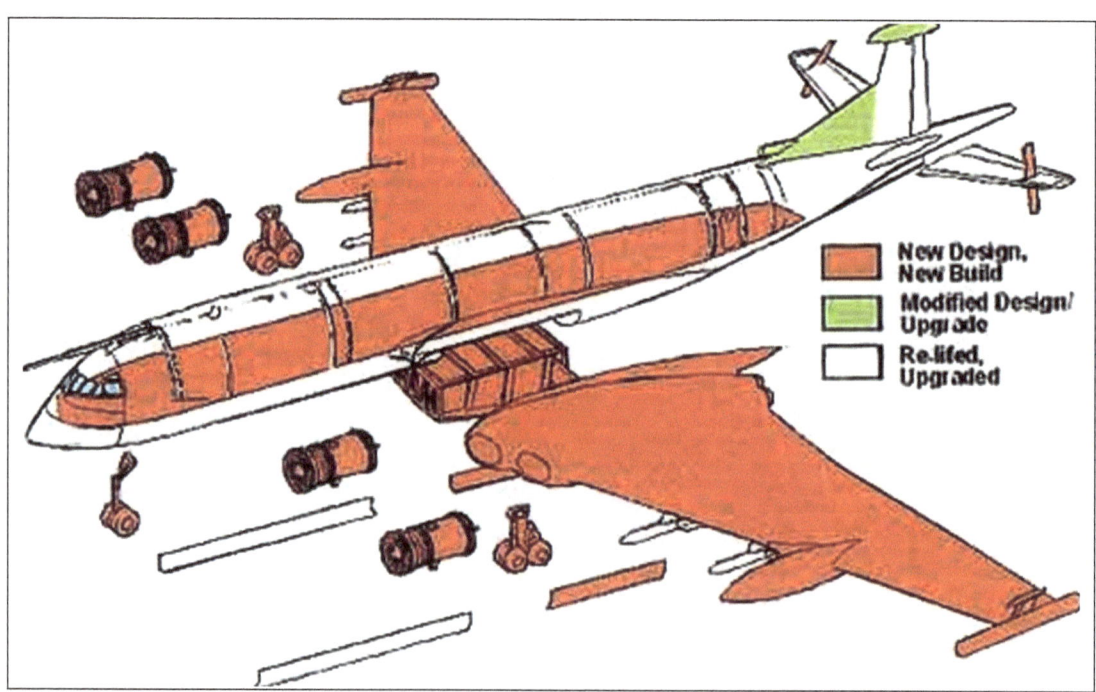

Diagram illustrating the areas of the new design/build, areas of modified design/build and upgraded areas carried over to the Nimrod 2000 (MRA4) from the Nimrod MR2. BAE Systems

The Nimrod 2000, renamed Nimrod MRA4 prior to actual build work commencing, was, in effect, to be developed as new build aircraft rather than a modified Nimrod MR2. Although some fuselage components and a few other components would be carried over from the earlier design, most of the structural components and systems were new (BAE Systems, 2002). The new build and refurbished Nimrod MR2 components were designed for a demanding fatigue and corrosion environment, building on decades of experience gained on legacy Nimrod flight operations. Increased (over legacy design) anti-corrosion protection was incorporated (BAE Systems, 2002), a necessity due to the high rate over water mission scenarios of the Nimrod 2000 (MRA4) concept.

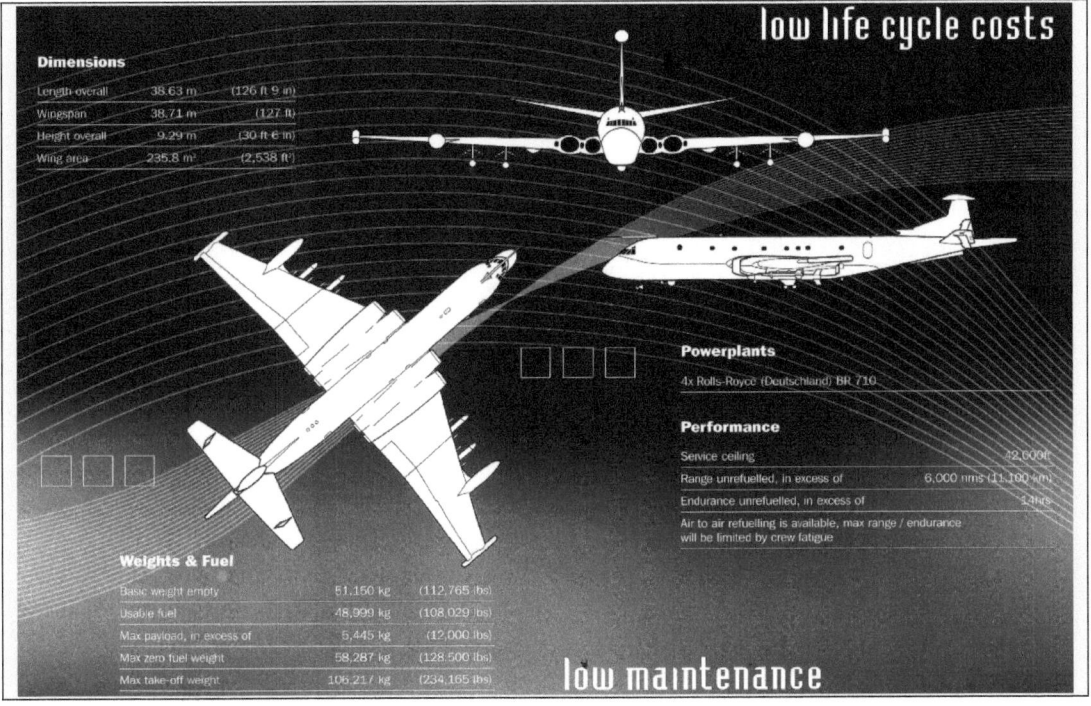

Three view general arrangement drawing of the Nimrod MRA4 (with tables detailing basic particulars) showing the basic outline identifiable as Nimrod lineage, along with redesigned and modified areas – wings and forward vertical tail assembly etc. BAE Systems

The primary operational requirements for the Nimrod MRA4, reaffirmed in 2002, was for a maritime patrol, reconnaissance, intelligence gathering strike platform to undertake anti-submarine warfare, anti-surface unit warfare, maritime reconnaissance/intelligence gathering and search and rescue missions. Each of the four main mission areas could be further broken down to sub-categories as follows. Anti-Submarine Warfare: 'Barrier search; Area Search; Datum search; Passive localisation; Active localisation; Classification and Tracking; Attack (Independent); Attack (Coordinated); Mast Search; C^{3}I [Command Control Communications and Intelligence]; Policing Patrol; Minelaying; Self-Defence' and 'Self Deployment' (BAE, 2002). Anti-Surface Unit Warfare: 'Barrier search; Area Search; Datum search; Tracking; Classification; Shadowing; Attack (Independent); Third Party Targeting; C^{3}I; Policing Patrol; Minelaying; Self-Defence' and 'Self Deployment' (BAE, 2002). Maritime Reconnaissance and Intelligence Gathering: 'Passive Search; Detection; Location; Collection; Evaluation; Classification; Shadowing; Processing' and 'C^{3}I' (BAE, 2002). Search and Rescue: 'Area Search; Datum Search; Beacon Search; SAR [Search and Rescue]; Escort; Combat SAR' and 'C^{3}I' (BAE, 2002). Secondary operational requirements were defined as patrolling the UK's Exclusive Economic Zone and assisting the civil authorities (BAE, 2002).

In 2003, it was envisioned that the Nimrod MRA4 would fulfill or contribute to the fulfillment of no less than 16 of the 27 military tasks then envisioned for the UK. Principal amongst these was MT26, protection of the UK's nuclear deterrent and MT8, maritime patrol, to preserve the integrity of UK maritime areas in a non-conflict period (PPR, 23.7.2003).

Nimrod MRA4 (Nimrod 2000) DIMENSIONS & WEIGHTS – The Nimrod MRA4 basic dimensions included a length of ~38.63 m (126 ft. 9 in); height overall, ~9.29 m (30 ft. 6 in) – a ~2.03 m increase over the ~9.06 m of the Nimrod MR2; wing span, ~38.71 m (127 ft.) – an increase of several feet over that of the Nimrod MR2, and wing area, ~235.8 m^2 (2,538 ft^2.), an increase on the ~197.047 m^2 (2,121 ft^2. of the MR2 (BAE). Weight came in at ~51150 kg (112,765 lb.), basic (operating) empty; Maximum unrefuelled weight, ~58287 kg (128,500 lb.); maximum take-off weight, ~106217 kg (234,165 lb.), of which maximum internal fuel mass was ~48999 kg (108,029 lb.) – a considerable increase on the ~38936 kg internal fuel carried by the Nimrod MR2 – and maximum payload, in excess of ~5443 kg (12,000 lb.), a small reduction over that of the Nimrod MR2 (BAE).

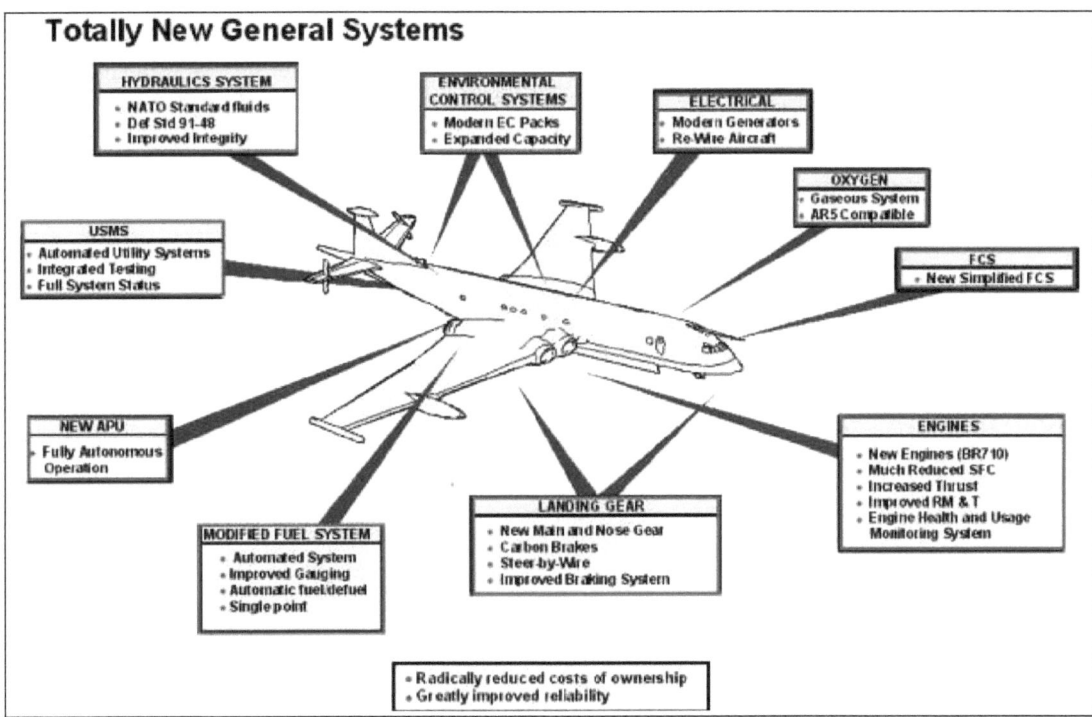

Top: Partial cutaway drawing of the Nimrod MRA4 (Nimrod 2000) illustrating the mission compartments with two assemblies of structures for the carriage of sonobouys and their launchers toward the rear of the aircraft. Bottom: Diagram illustrating Nimrod MRA4 (Nimrod 2000) new general systems BAE Systems

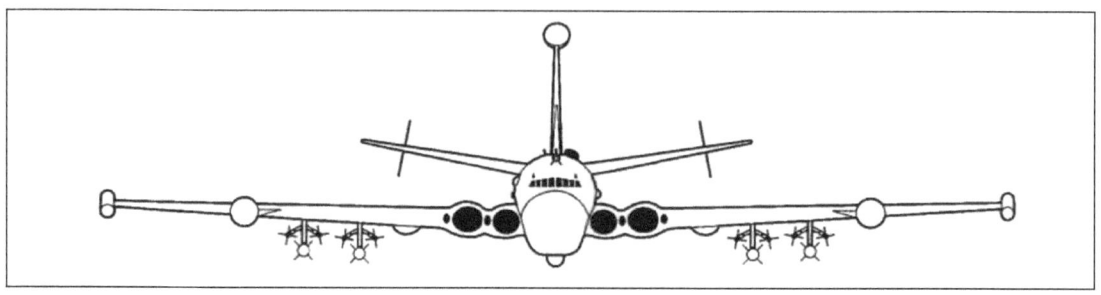

Forward view of the Nimrod MRA4 showing port main and nose wheel undercarriage units extended, with the starboard undercarriage unit ghosted.
BAE Systems

At the heart of the Nimrod MRA4 capabilities was the general and mission systems, which included the Utility Systems Management System, Navigation and Flight Management System, Engine Control System and Stores Management System.

USMS (Utility Systems Management System) – The USMS, incorporating an Automated Utility System with integrated testing capability, was designed to control, monitor and provide testing for a number of onboard aircraft systems: FCS (Flight Control System) – a new simplified FCS was developed for the Nimrod MRA4 – including the monitoring of aerodynamic surfaces; Undercarriage System, including overseeing the retraction and extraction process, steering for the nose wheel unit and brake pressures; Hydraulic System for the generation, protection and distribution of hydraulics – the Hydraulic System incorporated NATO Standard fluids, Def Std. 91-48, with improved integrity; The ECS (Environmental Control System), which oversaw cabin pressurisation and cooling – the ECS incorporated modern EC (Environmental Control) packs with expanded capacity; The fuel system unit oversaw gauging, management and fuel supply to the engines; The electrical supply system monitored, controlled and distributed aircraft electrical supply – electricals included a complete rewiring and incorporation of modern generators; Engine start-up and monitoring of the APU (Auxiliary Power Unit) – a new design integral APU was developed, allowing for fully autonomous operation, negating the requirement for ground power for start-up; 'Miscellaneous systems – ice and rain protection, life support, emergency equipment, fire protection, external lighting etc.' – the oxygen system incorporated an AR5 compatible gaseous system (BAE, 1996 & BAE, undated).

The Nimrod MRA4 was equipped with a new design main and nose undercarriage system, shown on PA02 during its maiden flight. BAE Systems

A new undercarriage design was incorporated to accommodate the increased maximum take-off and landing weights associated with the Nimrod MRA4 in comparison to those attainable with the MR2. The new undercarriage design incorporated improved capability main and nose gear units, with carbon brakes for the improved braking system and steer-by-wire for the nose wheel unit (BAE). The four wheel main undercarriage units retracted to lay in the wing, housed in a large ventral wing fairing when fully retracted. The twin nose-wheel unit retracted aft to lay in the forward fuselage underside, below the cockpit section.

The Rolls Royce BR710 turbofan engines were the most prominent of the new design general systems incorporated into the Nimrod MRA4. The new engines were expected to provide around 30% more thrust than that provided by the Rolls Royce Spey engines installed in the Nimrod MR2, whilst burning around 25% less fuel. Adoption of the new engines was expected to increase operational range and time on station and improve air base performance.

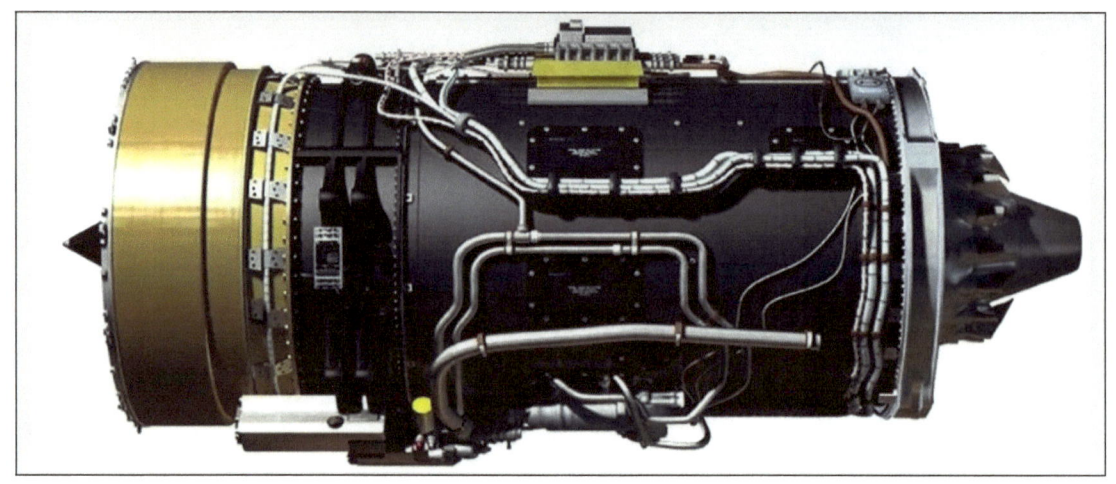

Rolls Royce (Germany) BR710 turbofan engine. Rolls Royce Germany

The BR710 was developed under the core BR700 program, with low noise emission as a major design driver, this being significantly quieter than the Rolls Royce Spey engine installed in the Nimrod MR2. The low noise emissions, in comparison to legacy engines, would facilitate the ability to operate from and transit through air base/airports across the world (RR, 2020). As well as low external noise emissions, the BR710 low noise emission reduced the Nimrod MRA4 internal noise levels (BAE Systems, 2002), improving the crew operating environment. The engine was developed for operations in a number of environmental conditions, including hot and or high basing locations (RR, 2020).

The BR710 engine incorporated a new design utilities sub-system, improving overall performance and increasing mission functionality, whilst providing reliability levels associated with civil airliners and reduced operating costs (BAE, 2002). Reducing operating costs was a program goal, which would be further contributed to through the BR710 engine being designed for significantly reduced specific fuel consumption over the legacy Spey engines installed in the Nimrod MR2. This met the Nimrod MRA4 requirement for high speed transit to patrol areas over the weather in long-range flight whilst carrying a large stores load, and enabled long duration flights to be conducted at upper altitudes. The engine was designed with high performance in take-off and climb out to cruise altitude – intended as, or in excess of, the efficiency available in modern civil airliners (RR, 2020). Whilst oft stated claims that the Nimrod MRA4 would be the only maritime patrol aircraft to be powered by jet engines was inaccurate, it was clear that the jet power would bestow upon the design the ability to transit to a designated patrol area at higher speed and altitudes than turboprop contempories and provide more timely response to time critical missions, such as search and rescue operations.

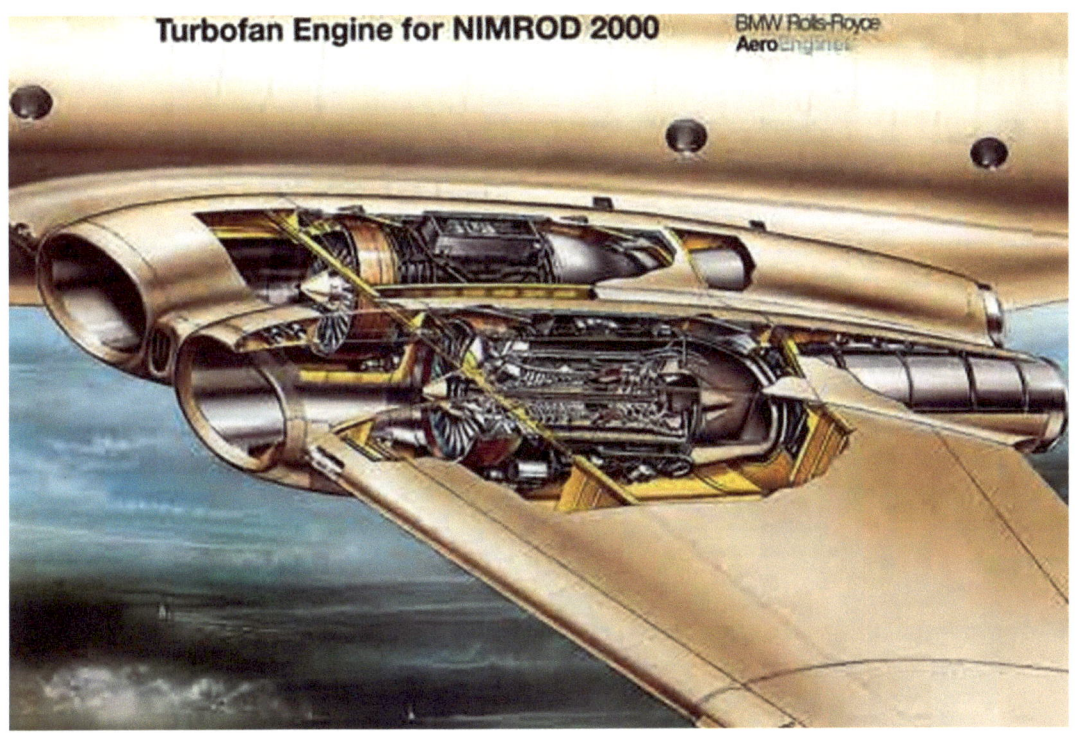

Diagram showing a cutaway illustration of the Nimrod 2000 (MRA4) port engine bays and the arrangement of the BMW Rolls Royce Aero Engines (Rolls Royce Germany) BR710 turbofan engines. Rolls Royce Germany

The BR710 was designed with an integral HUMS (Health and Usage Monitoring System) and incorporated a FADEC (Full Authority Digital Engine Control System) developed by RoSEC. The FADEC, which weighed in at ~9.1 kg (20 lb.), provisioned for a high degree of functionality through its dual channel architecture; and the HUMS provided for extensive detection of faults (BAE Systems, 1996).

Prior to selection for and flight in the Nimrod MRA4, BR710 variants had been cleared for operations at ratings between ~6697 kg (14,750 lb.) and ~7031 kg (15,500 lb.) thrust (RR, 2020). The variant powering the Nimrod MRA4 was apparently cleared to operate at power settings up to ~8391 kg (18500 lb.) – actual ratings achieved in flight test would have fluctuated from this value (Harkins, 2004). The first run of a BR710 engine had been conducted in 1994. In November of the following year, flight testing commenced on a Gulfstream V (G550) biz-jet class aircraft. Certification for operation was received in August 1996 and the first flight of a Global Express aircraft powered by BR710 was conducted in October that year. Certification of specific serial BR710 engines was received in January 1997 (RR, 2020) and they were proven in operation of Bombardier Global 5000, Global 6000 and Gulfstream G500 and G550 civil biz-jet class aircraft fleets.

The BR710 engines were larger than the Spey's installed in the Nimrod MR2, necessitating the adoption of larger engine nacelles. This resulted in increased wing area in the new design/build wings, which had the benefit of facilitating increased accommodation of internal fuel capacity. The Nimrod MRA4 also incorporated a new centre wing box, new weapons bay doors, modified wingtip sections (to accommodate new Electronic Sensor measures pods), larger finlets on the horizontal tail-plane (carried over from the Nimrod MR2) and significant structural changes to elements of the rear fuselage/tail section. Whilst the main vertical tail surface was carried over from the Nimrod MR2, the fairing at the top (enlarged to house a new decoy system) and the tapered base unit were extensively modified, the latter section housing elements of the Environmental Control System (Harkins, 2004).

Adoption of the BR710 engine for Nimrod MRA4 resulted in the aircraft engine nacelles being enlarged (previous page) in comparison to the Nimrod MR2/R1 engine nacelles (this page top). The Nimrod inflight refueling system was refurbished and carried over from the legacy Nimrod fleet **(Nimrod R1 illustrated) this page bottom.** BAE Systems/Crown Copyright

Modified Fuel System – The refueling system for the MRA4 was of a new design, employing only a marginal percentage of components from the Nimrod MR2, all of which were refurbished prior to incorporation into the MRA4 (Hansard, 2007 & BAE). The new/modified system featured full automation with single-point ground refuelling, improved gauging and automatic fuelling/de-fuelling (BAE).

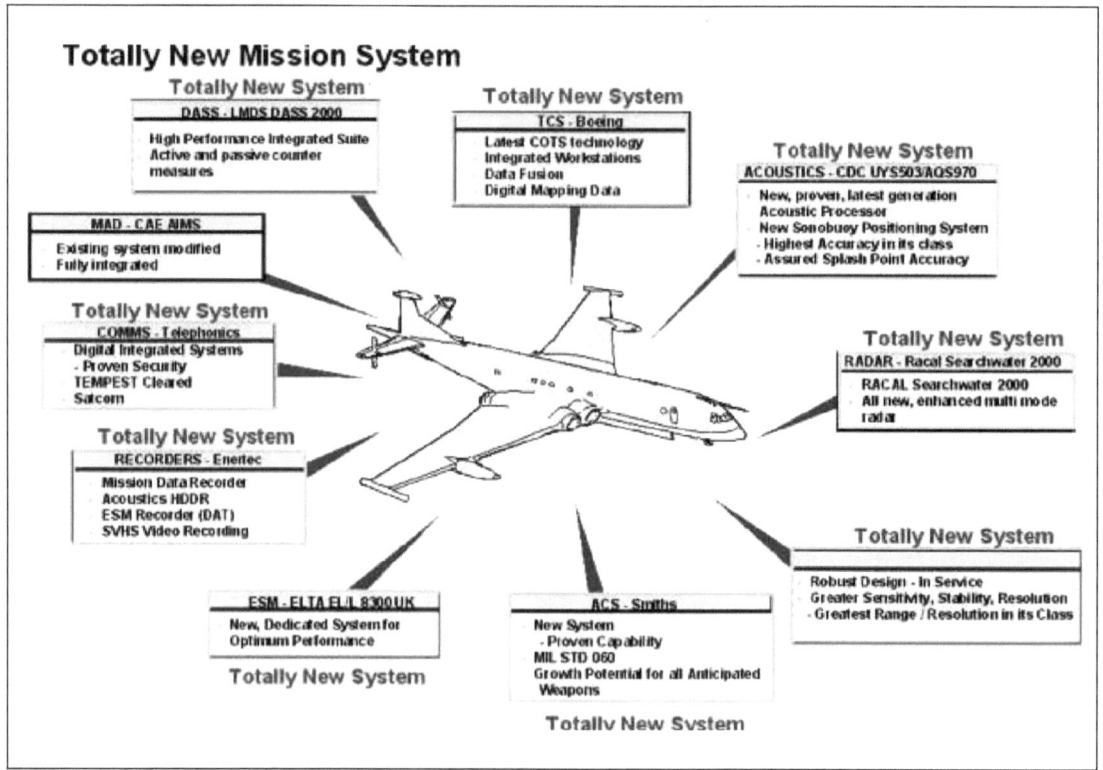

Diagram illustrating the new mission systems specified for the Nimrod MRA4. BAE Systems

Avionics & Mission Systems – The Nimrod MRA4 was equipped with new design fourth generation avionics/sensors (BAE, 2004 & BAE, 2002a). The sensor suite provided the capability for detection, identification, by class, and tracking of surface and sub surface marine vessels. Sensor sensitivity was optimised for detection of small targets moving at high speed in water types ranging from Open Ocean to littoral. The ability to detect small objects was central to the search and rescue mission, allowing location of life rafts and even persons in the water (NAO MPR, 2009).

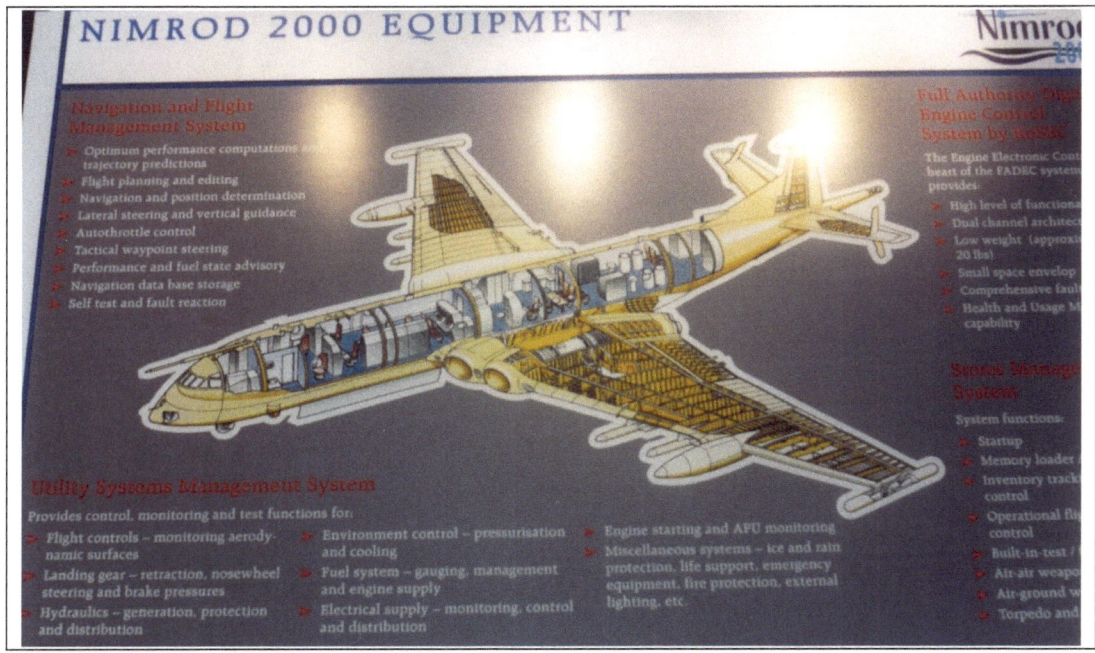

Nimrod 2000 (MRA4) diagram with an overview of the aircraft Utility Systems Management, Navigation and Flight Management, Full Authority Digital Engine Control and the Stores Management Systems. Author

System integration was on a large scale and included: in excess of six million lines of software code; installation and operation of 90 antennas and sensors; in excess of 1,000 Line Replaceable Units for avionics and mission systems and extensive use of COTS (Commercial Off The Shelf) items (BAE, 2004, BAE, 2002 & BAE, 2002a).

When developed, the Nimrod MRA4 mission system was, in terms of functionality and capability, among, if not, the most advanced in the world. The system was designed with growth potential to facilitate adaption to changing threat environments and technology advances, allowing integration of new systems as required (BAE, 2002).

Specifics of the mission systems included: the Tactical Command System, with considerable data handling capability and dual redundancy; open systems architecture, featuring shared/appropriated processing; Searchwater 2000 multi-mode radar complex; up to date acoustic system, incorporating an accurate sonobuoy positioning system; Electro-Optical Surveillance Detection System; integrated MAD (Magnetic Anomaly Detector); an Electronic Surveillance Measures complex; Defensive Aids Sub-System and Wide-ranging secure communications and data-link systems (BAE, 2002).

The mission deck in the main cabin of Nimrod MRA4 PA02, the second development Nimrod MRA4. BAE Systems

Avionics Systems & Flight Deck – Advances in technology facilitated a two-crew flight deck (reduced from three in the Nimrod MR2) dominated by modern avionics systems developed through the technology base(s) for the Airbus and Eurofighter Typhoon programs.

Dominating the flight deck was the EFIS (Electronic Flight Instrumentation System), incorporating a grouping of seven full-colour liquid crystal multi-function display screens. Major components of the avionics suite included the Automatic Flight Control System; the Accurate Navigation/Flight Management System and the Ground Proximity Warning System (BAE, 2002). Mission and flight data could be accessed and stored by an Enertec mission recorder suite, which consisted of an MDR (Mission Data Recorder), Acoustic HDDR, Electronic Sensor (Surveillance) Measures recorder (DAT) and SVHS Video Recorder (BAE).

Navigation and Flight Management System – When the Nimrod 2000 program was authorised in July 1996, the specified navigation and flight management system was intended to perform a number of mission functions: compute optimum performance and trajectory predictions; conduct planning and data editing for the flight profile; flight navigation of and determination of aircraft position; provision for steering laterally and guidance in the vertical plane; provide automatic throttle control; waypoint steering; advise on aircraft performance and fuel status; database storage of navigation data and a self-test and reaction to discovered fault(s) function (BAE Systems, 1996).

For the primary anti-submarine warfare mission, the Nimrod MRA4 was equipped with acoustic and MAD systems. The acoustics suite, employed primarily for sub-surface vessel detection, was centred on a CDC UYS503/AQS-970 complex featuring then current generation acoustic processor(s) with a sonobuoy positioning system for sonobuoy deployment, featuring the high accuracy then available with an assured splash (sea surface impact) accuracy (BAE). The CAF NMS MAD was carried over from the Nimrod MR2, but modified to incorporate technology advances for service in the Nimrod MRA4 (BAE). The MAD, which was mounted in an elongated boom in the extreme tail of the aircraft, was employed to detect and localise changes in the Earth's magnetic field, which could confirm the presence of a large metallic object, such as a submarine under the sea/ocean surface. The effectiveness of such systems had been significantly reduced through incorporation of external coatings on modern submarines designed to hinder the detectability by MAD.

The Magnetic Anomaly Detector, housed in an elongated boom extending aft from the aircraft tail section, was carried over from the Nimrod MR2, but modified to incorporate technology advances for service in the Nimrod MRA4. BAE Systems

Radar – The new generation Nimrod mission systems included the newly developed RACAL Searchwater 2000 enhanced multi-mode radar complex, featuring significantly enhanced sensitivity and enhanced range/resolution compared with legacy systems (BAE). Searchwater 2000, which featured a large area antenna to facilitate the enhancement in detection range, was developed as a Pulse Doppler multi-mode radar system of high power output to facilitate multiple functions at long range. Developed for the Nimrod MRA4, the system was subsequently adapted to Searchwater 2000AEW (Airborne Early Warning) standard to equip the Westland Sea King AEW MK 7 helicopter (Thales, 2001).

Searchwater 2000 incorporated a MK XII Identification Friend or Foe interrogator system, inherent Electronic Sensor Measures and INS/GPS (Inertial Navigation System/Global Positioning System) navigation complex. The radar could provide over the horizon targeting capability for the Nimrods own weapons or weapons launched from other platforms (Thales, 2001).

Searchwater 2000MR incorporated a Moving Target Indicator mode and a number of maritime operating modes optimised for anti-submarine warfare /anti-surface unit warfare missions in littoral waters and in Open Ocean. Navigation ground mapping modes could be advanced to provide target classification, weather observance and beacon functions. The littoral surveillance mode and pulse-Doppler overland tracking modes facilitated the detection of small targets, such as a submarine periscope (in sea surveillance mode), even when subjected to sea/land background clutter. The radar was capable of discrimination between high speed airborne targets and slower moving land and sea surface targets. The Searchwater 2000AEW air to air modes included look-up & look-down (Thales, 2001), this being carried over from the Searchwater 2000MR developed for Nimrod MRA4.

The Searchwater 2000MR radar complex was housed in the aircraft nose section, with much of the Elta developed EL/L8300UK electronic sensor measures suite housed in wingtip mounted fixtures. BAE Systems-Helen Stansfield

Electro-Optical Surveillance and Detection – Complementing the radar was an advanced Electro-Optical Surveillance and Detection system, mounted on the aircraft undersurface. This complex was designed to provision high-resolution imagery for search, identification and intelligence gathering in passive (non-emission emitting) mode, reducing the Nimrod MRA4 reliance on radar (which would betray the aircraft presence through emitting radio frequency (radiation) waves) for detecting air and surface objects.

Electronic sensor measures capability was centred on the Elta EL/L8300UK electronic sensor measures suite (BAE) – this system had previously been selected for incorporation into the upgrade of Australian P-3 maritime patrol aircraft. The Electronic sensor measures suite would enable electronic transmissions to be detected, localised and classified, enhancing the Nimrod MRA4's considerable surveillance capability already inherent in other systems, such as the radar complex.

Defensive Aids Sub-System – The DASS 2000 Defensive Aids Sub-System was developed as a high performance integrated suite of defensive aids, incorporating active and passive countermeasures, including a Radar Warning Receiver to warn of radio frequency threats (BAE). The self-protection capability was to be extensive in order to meet an initial requirement for out of area operations where the aircraft could potentially be exposed to modern advanced capability air defence systems (BAE, 2002). This would have required a radar jamming and deployable countermeasures, such as chaff and flare systems to reduce the threat. However, as the program progressed, reductions in self-defence capability resulted in the Nimrod MRA4 being defined as having diminished ability to operate in a threat environment (NAO, 2010). This would have limited it to local operations in the event of war with a major power, such as the Russian Federation.

The communications suite included digital integrated systems with enhanced security and TEMPEST cleared SATCOM (Satellite Communications) system (BAE). The communication suite would have provisioned for the Nimrod MRA4 to communicate over all bands, ranging from low frequency to ultra-high frequency. The satellite communication system was designed for global secure commination. A secure data-link was specified, increasing the aircraft net-centric warfare capability through facilitating the exchange of tactical data with other airborne platforms and surface stations.

Arguably the heart of the Nimrod MRA4 mission capability, the Boeing developed Tactical Command System incorporated new generation COTS for the crew integrated workstations, with digital mapping data and data fusion between the various mission systems

(BAE). Crew requirements were reduced from thirteen in the Nimrod MR2 to ten in the MRA4 (this included two flight crew) (PPR, 23.7.2003). This reduction in crew complement was facilitated through increased mission and flight systems automation (NAO MPR, 1997).

Early artist rendering of the Nimrod 2000 (with representative Nimrod MR2 layout) launching a cruise missile over rough sea. BAE Systems

Stores Management System – The Stores Management System provided a number of functions: 'Startup; Memory Loader …; Inventory tracking control; Operational flight control'; Built-in test capability; Air to air weapon; air to ground weapon and torpedo and mine employment (BAE, 1996). The carriage and employment of stores and ordnance by the Nimrod MRA4 would be controlled by the integrated Smiths Armament Control System, which was centred on a MIL STD 060 databus, facilitating integration of new weapon systems as they became available. The system oversaw the carriage and release of stores, which could be carried in the large internal weapons bay and on wing stations (BAE, 2004, BAE, 2002 & BAE, 2002a).

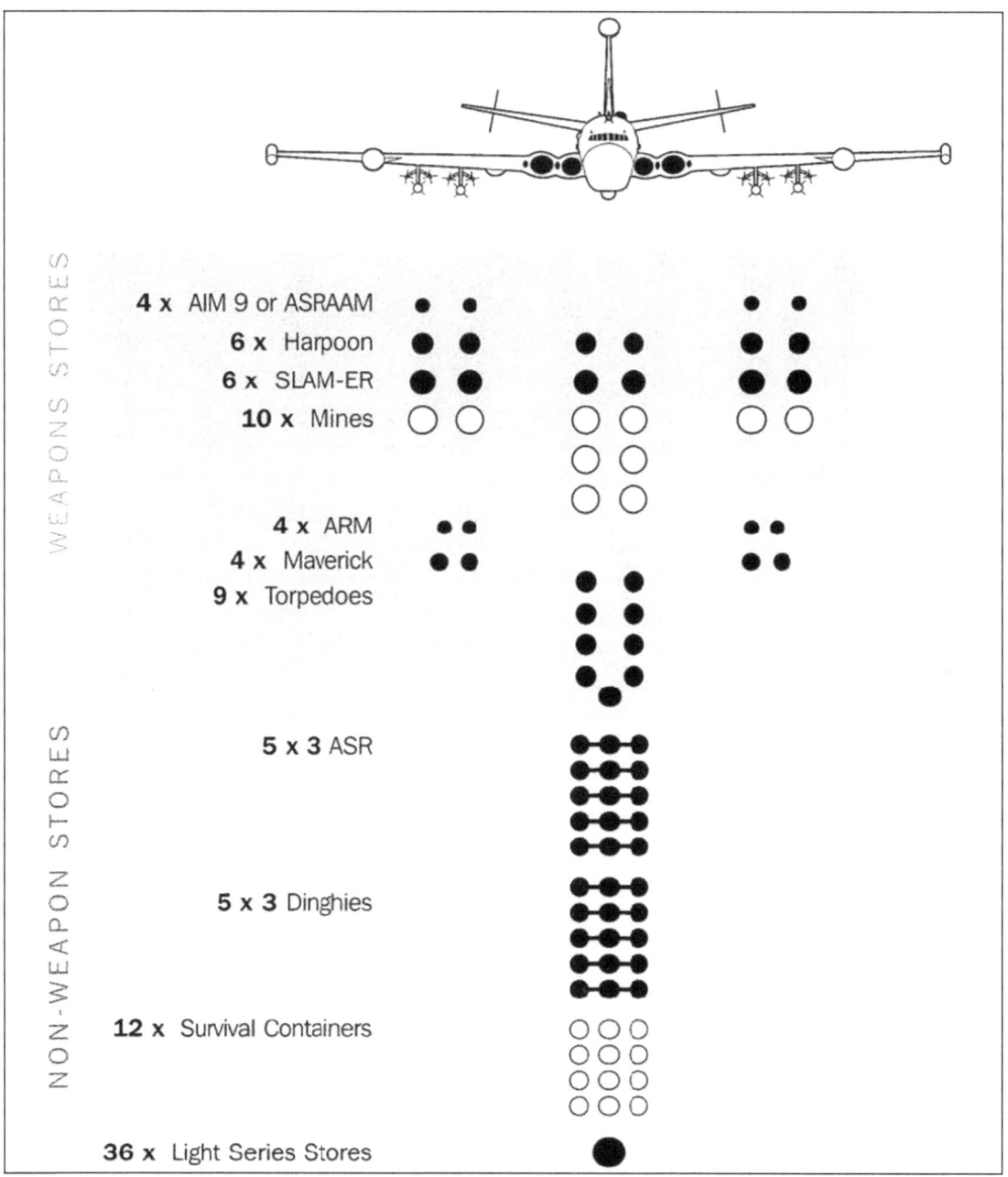

Diagram illustrating the stores potential of the Nimrod MRA4 as of 2002. A maximum of twelve missiles could be carried. Whilst the diagram text states that a maximum of four AIM-9 or ASRAAM could be carried, the diagram graphic suggests eight such weapons (four was the specified number) in addition to the 6 x AGM-84. BAE Systems

Although not fully defined, in 2002 the stores carriage for the Nimrod MRA4 included a number of options. Weapon options included: Sting

Ray torpedo (nine carried in the internal weapons bay); mines (6 housed in the internal weapons bay and four carried on the wing stores carriage stations); AGM-84 Harpoon anti-ship missile (2 housed in the internal weapons bays and 4 carried on the wing stations); AGM-84H SLAM ER (Stand-Off Land Attack Missile Enhanced Response) (2 housed in the internal weapons bays and 4 carried on the wing stations); AIM-9L/M infrared or ASRAAM (Advanced Short Range Air to Air Missile) IIR (Imaging Infrared) guided short-range air to air missiles (4 carried on the wing stations); ALARM (Air Launched Anti-Radiation Missile) (4 carried on the wing stations) or AGM-65 Maverick short-range air to surface missiles (4 carried on the wing stations) (BAE, 2002).

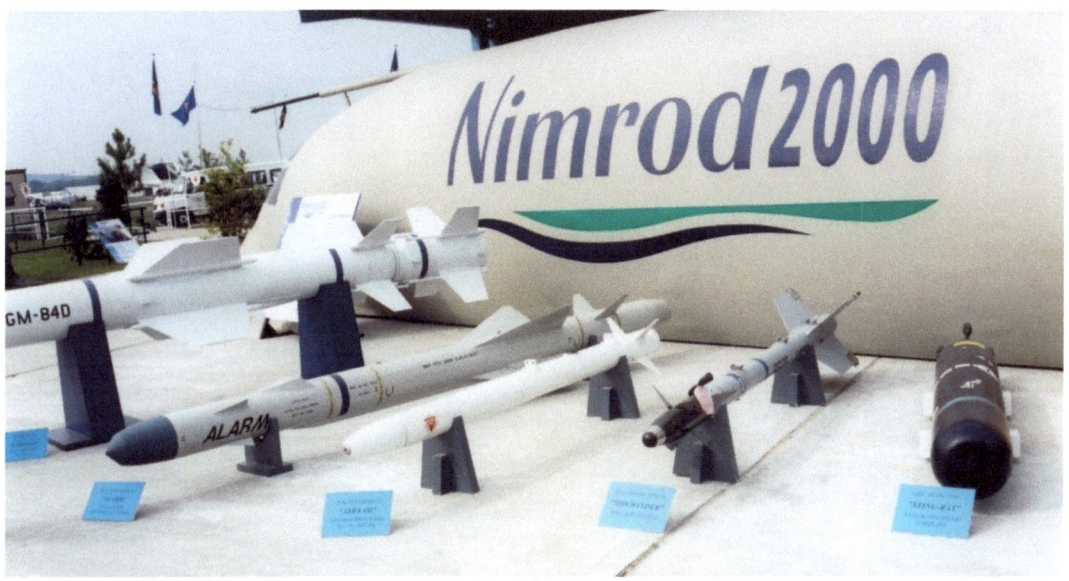

Nimrod 2000 exhibition at the Farnborough International trade show in September 1996, showing a plethora of potential weaponry – right to left: Sting Ray lightweight torpedo, AIM-9 Sidewinder infrared guided air to air missile, Advanced Short Range Air to Air Missile, Air Launched Anti-Radiation Missile and AGM-84D (with surface launch RGM booster extension) anti-ship cruise missile. Author

STING RAY – Considering the primary maritime patrol/anti-submarine warfare mission, the primary weapon specified for the Nimrod MRA4 was the Sting Ray Mod 1 air launched anti-submarine torpedo. This was an update of the Sting Ray Mod 0 weapon that had armed the Nimrod MR2. Sting Ray had been developed during the 1970's as a counter to increased capabilities inherent in the then latest generation of Soviet submarines that possessed faster submerged operating speeds and could dive deeper than previous generation vessels, posing difficulties for existing NATO anti-submarine warfare weapons. The new generation of Soviet boats also incorporated double hull construction, which bestowed a degree of protection from legacy service torpedoes. When it entered service, the Marconi Sting Ray was arguably the most advanced weapon in its class, offering greater operational depths compared to its predecessor, the United States MK44 (a standard NATO weapon then in service).

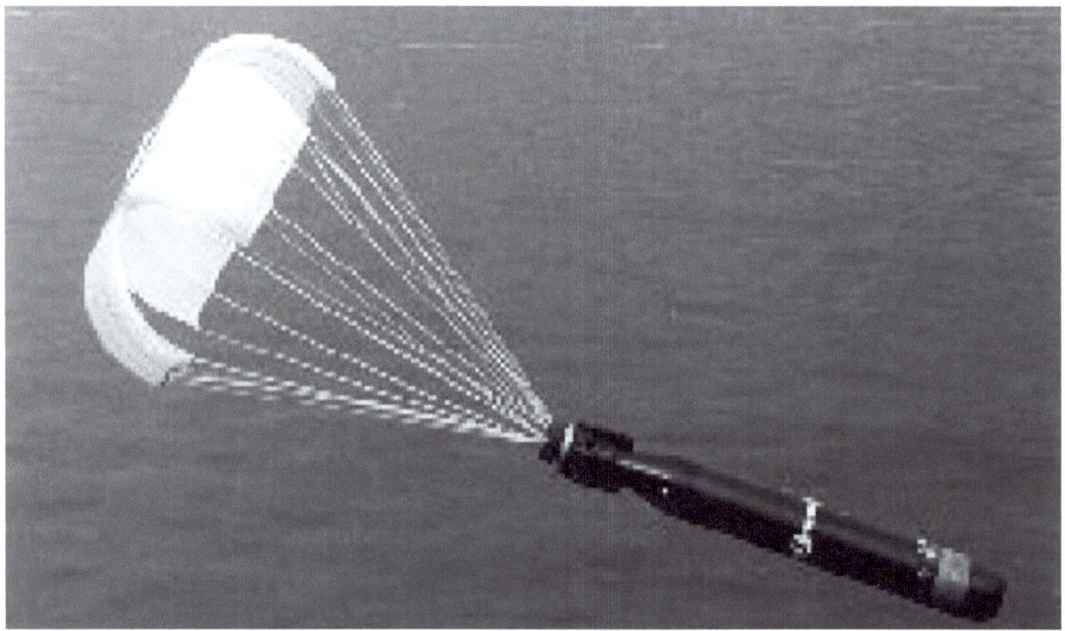

Sting Ray was air dropped from Nimrod, its free fall retarded by deployment of a parachute system, jettisoned before it entered the water. UK Gov.

The on-board digital computer, coupled with a multi-mode, multi-beam active/passive sonar, facilitated the ability for Sting Ray to conduct repeat attacks on a manoeuvring target. The weapon was propelled by an electrical driven pump jet with a sea water activated battery, which ensured that there was minimal to no loss of speed with increasing depth. In order to deal with the double hull submarine construction target sets Sting Ray was armed with a directed energy shaped charge warhead, designed to penetrate both the outer and inner hulls.

Although still undergoing trials Sting Ray was taken to the South Atlantic during the 1982 Falklands War, but was not used operationally. Full service entry with the Royal Navy and RAF was achieved in 1983.

Sting Ray Mod 0 Lightweight Torpedo

Length: ~2.6 m (102.25 in)
Diameter: ~0.3 m (12.75 in)
Weight: ~265 kg (585 lb.)
Speed: ~83 km/h (45 knots)
Range: ~11100 m (36,417 ft.)
Diving depth: 800 m
Warhead: ~40 kg (88 lb.) shaped charge high explosive

Potential alternatives to the SRLE included the A.244/S Mod.1 lightweight anti-submarine torpedo Author

As a principal armament for the RAF's replacement for the Nimrod MR2, Sting Ray was to be developed under the SRLE (Sting Ray Life Extension) capability upgrade program, intended to remain in service until around 2025 when it would be replaced by a new lightweight torpedo developed under international competition/cooperation (NAO, 2006). The SRLE was authorised in May 1995 and GEC-Marconi Underwater Systems moved from the feasibility phase to award of a full development contract in July 1996, the same month that the Nimrod 2000 was selected as the preferred Nimrod MR2 replacement. This was followed by design certification approval, approval for SRLE manufacturing and award of a contract to BAE Systems (GEC-Marconi Underwater Systems amalgamated with British Aerospace to form BAE Systems in 1999) on 30 January 2003 (NAO, 2006 & NAO, 1999).

Sting Ray Mod1. BAE Systems

The program initially called for retaining the warhead of the Sting Ray Mod 0. In response to a new safety policy, an new insensitive munition warhead was specified for the SRLE in February 2001. This program was later deferred from implementation in the SRLE program, but retained as a separate program (NAO, 2006).

Completion of SRLE production qualification trials in December 2005 paved the way for delivery of the first serial updated Sting Ray torpedo in February 2006, with an initial operational capability (in-service date) declared in June that year (NAO, 2006). Sting Ray Mod 1 was also selected by Norway to meet its advanced lightweight anti-submarine torpedo requirement (BAE, 2018 & BAE, 2011).

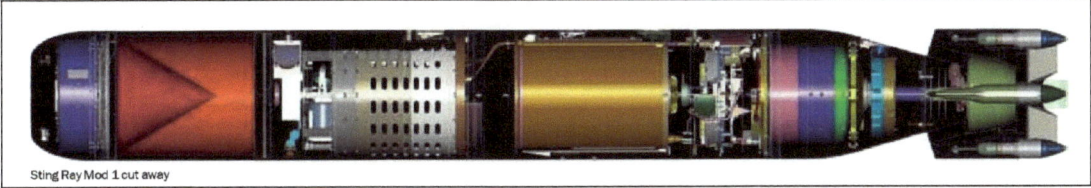

Ghosted cutaway drawing showing the internal compartments of the Sting Ray Mod 1. BAE Systems

The two major program goals were introduction of software driven capability enhancements to effect increased Sting Ray Mod 1 effectiveness against then modern submarine designs and lower life cycle costs through introducing a maintenance free storage concept. The new software, tactical and acoustic, was developed through analysis of data that had been gleaned from operation of the Sting Ray Mod 0 trials in water. New technology advances were incorporated into the operating algorithms, both tactical and processing. It was hardware modifications that were most notable, in particular the new design frontal array. The torpedo incorporated a new navigation complex, digital signal processing and guidance computers – embracing COTS components – and new design motor control system and electro-mechanical actuation system to drive/control the torpedo control/manoeuvring surfaces. Components of the homing system of the Sting Ray Mod 0 were completely replaced in the Sting Ray Mod 1. The new signal processor, capable of performing 'advanced classification algorithms', was developed to enable the torpedo to better classify the target against non-target returns, such as natural formations on the sea bed and marine fauna (BAE, 2018 & BAE, 2011).

The electro-hydraulic servo-system of the Sting Ray Mod 0 was superseded by an electro-mechanical actuation system in the Sting Ray Mod 1. The main power plant of the Sting Ray Mod 1 was a magnesium/silver chloride battery, incorporating a sea water electrolyte.

The improved capability autopilot was designed to enable the torpedo to operate efficiently in shallow/littoral waters through incorporation of 'complex tactical software routines' – the autopilot complex could receive increased levels of data supplied by the launch platform (Nimrod MRA4) compared to the Sting Ray Mod 0 autopilot (BAE, 2018 & BAE, 2011).

Sting Ray Mod 1 was designed for operation from multiple platforms, including helicopter, as illustrated here. BAE Systems

The guidance/homing system provisioned for accurate delivery of the warhead to a position close to incidence (movement in a straight line) in comparison to the target submarine pressure hull, to facilitate the optimum likelihood of target destruction. The new insensitive munition shaped charge warhead had been specified for the Sting Ray Mod 1 to increase lethality against the hardened and double hulled submarine targets. This enhanced lethality would have been provisioned through delivering an isotropic blast wave, the target being penetrated by the shaped charge directing a molten metal jet designed to compromise the integrity of the pressure hull, resulting in catastrophic pressure hull pressure loss (BAE, 2018 & BAE, 2011).

The Sting Ray Mod 1 incorporated a modern solid-state inertial measurement unit, which, combined with the tactical software modes, reduced vulnerability to advanced acoustic countermeasures (BAE, 2018 & BAE, 2011).

The incorporated capability enhancements increased the weapons effectiveness against high speed, deep submerging submarines and conventional powered submarines operating in coastal waters or open sea/ocean (BAE, 2018 & BAE, 2011).

The Nimrod MR4 retained the copious elongated stores bay of the Nimrod MR2 (illustrated). The bay could house a variety of stores options ranging from torpedoes to rescue equipment. Author

The Nimrod MR2 could potentially carry unguided 454 kg (1,000 lb.) class high explosive unguided bombs. There was no requirement to carry this over to the Nimrod MRA4. While not a specified capability requirement, Nimrod MRA4 had the potential to be configured as a long-range stand-off strike platform armed with MBDA Storm Shadow subsonic cruise missiles, which had a launch range in the region of 250 km. As noted above, BAE Systems documentation outlined the potential for Nimrod MRA4 to carry and launch up to six AGM-84H SLAM ER, but this weapon was not specified for the Nimrod fleet intended to operate with the RAF. In the event, the only cruise missile armament that was specified to arm Nimrod MRA4 was the Block II AGM-84 Harpoon subsonic anti-ship cruise missile, in a similar capacity to that of the Nimrod MR2/Harpoon combination. The AGM-84 had been procured as an armament option for the RAF Nimrod MR2 fleet in the early 1980's. Clearance of the weapon for deployment was accelerated during the Falklands War of April-June 1982, but the weapon was not operational prior to the ceasefire than brought active combat operations to an end on 14 June that year.

Harpoon had been designed/developed from the late 1960s, when the USN had a requirement for an anti-ship missile with a 92.5 km range. The concept emerged as an extreme low altitude (so called sea skimming), active radar guided missile for attacks against slow manoeuvring maritime targets at considerable distance from the launch platform. The surface launched UGM-84 entered service in 1977. An air launched variant was developed for employment from United States Air Force Boeing B-52 Stratofortress strategic bomber/missile carrier aircraft (entered service on the B-52 in 1983) (Boeing, 2018) and USN P-3 Orion maritime patrol aircraft. The Nimrod MR2 was not an ideal platform for attacking heavily defended targets due to deficiencies in self defence capability. This was deemed an acceptable drawback, which would, in part, be overcome by the AGM-84 stand-off launch capability, which merited its employment when the Nimrod could launch its missile(s) from outside the target area effective air defence engagement zone.

RGM-84L Block II Harpoon, representative of the AGM-84, but with the surface launch booster section added at the rear. Author

The Nimrod MRA4 was to be armed with Block II AGM-84L (initially the AGM-84D was associated with the Nimrod 2000 future armament options) for anti-surface unit warfare operations. As noted above, some BAE Systems documentation referred to the AGM-84H SLAM ER as an armament option for the Nimrod MRA4. The potential of the Nimrod MRA4 to evolve into a land attack platform with a significant stand-off capability could have been met through integration of the MBDA Storm Shadow stand-off cruise missile as noted above. However, there was never any official requirement for Storm Shadow integration on Nimrod, which would eventually have the requirement for operations in a high threat environment omitted from the program goals.

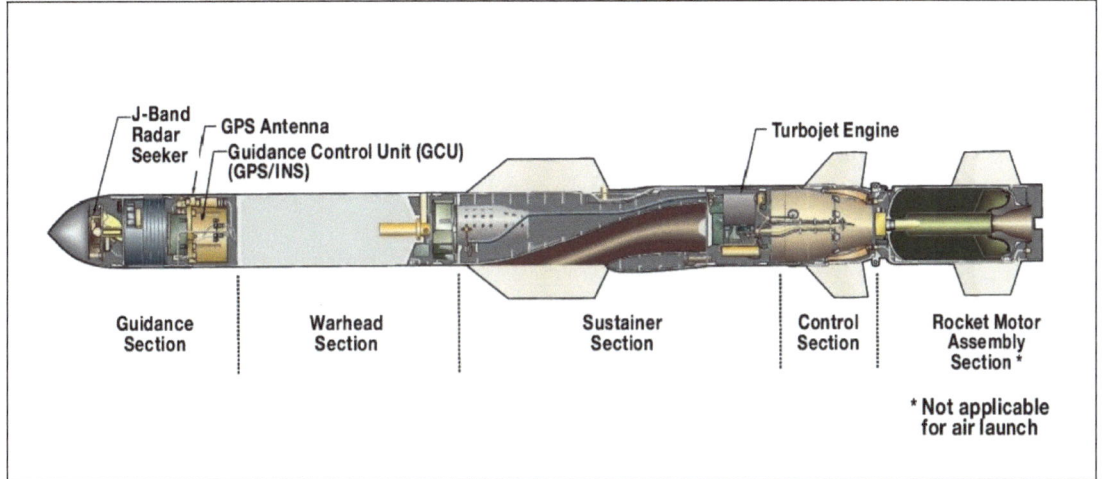

Cutaway diagram of the Block II AGM-84 Harpoon, illustrating the various missile sections. Boeing

A quasi-land attack capability would have been inherent in the Block II AGM-84, which was capable of fully autonomous over the horizon strike against sea surface or land targets in environmental conditions of fair or adverse weather. The GPS aided inertial navigation guidance system provisioned for precision strike against targets, which would be destroyed or disabled by the integral ~227 kg (500 lb.) blast fragmentation warhead (Boeing, 2018).

The Block II Harpoon assembly consisted of, fore to aft: the guidance section; warhead; sustainer; control and rocket motor assembly sections – the latter section was omitted in the air launched variant(s). The guidance section accommodated the J-band radar seeker head, the GPS antenna and the GPS/INS guidance control complex. The warhead section was located behind the guidance section, with the sustainer section – accommodating the turbojet cruise engine – located aft of the warhead section at the missile rear, followed by the rocket motor assembly in the RGM-84/UGM-84 (Boeing, 2018).

> AGM-84/RGM-84/UGM-84 – data furnished by Boeing
>
> Propulsion: Air breathing turbojet cruise engine (RGM/UGM-84 adds a solid-propellant booster)
> Diameter: 13.5 in (~34.3 cm)
> Length: 151.5 in (~385 cm)
> Weight: 1,160 lb. (~526 kg) for air launch variant
> Range: In excess of 67 nm (~124 km)
> Speed: Classified. Estimated to be in the region of Mach 0.75-0.85
> Warhead: 500 lb. (~227 kg) class penetration high explosive blast fragmentation
> Guidance: Midcourse global positioning system/inertial navigation and active radar homing in the terminal phase

Artist depiction of a Block II AGM-84, launched from a USN Boeing P-8 Poseidon maritime patrol aircraft. Boeing

Air to Air – Integration of the AIM-9L/M infrared guided air to air missile as an operational weapon was unlikely post 2003, as Nimrod MRA4, had it attained operational status, would have done so as the last remaining tactical aircraft carrier platforms for Sidewinder were nearing retirement from RAF service. The MBDA ASRAAM would have formed the primary air to air armament, had an air to air capability been progressed with, as this missile was a generation ahead of the AIM-9L/M in capability and featured enhanced range.

The requirement for an air to air missile capability for the Nimrod fleet had emerged following a 12 May 1982 encounter between a Nimrod MR2 from No.201 Squadron RAF and an Argentine air force Boeing 707 derived maritime reconnaissance aircraft over the South Atlantic at the time of the Falklands War. As the Nimrod had no air to air weapons it was powerless to attack the Argentine aircraft, which was not closed on (this encounter was outside the British imposed Total Exclusion Zone around the Falkland Islands, therefore, even an armed Nimrod would may not have been authorised to press an attack). This encounter contributed to the Ministry of Defence decision to install four AIM-9 missiles on wing stores stations of Nimrods involved in patrols over the South Atlantic. With this weapon fit the Nimrods would have theoretically been able to intercept Argentine aircraft encountered, although no further such encounters occurred.

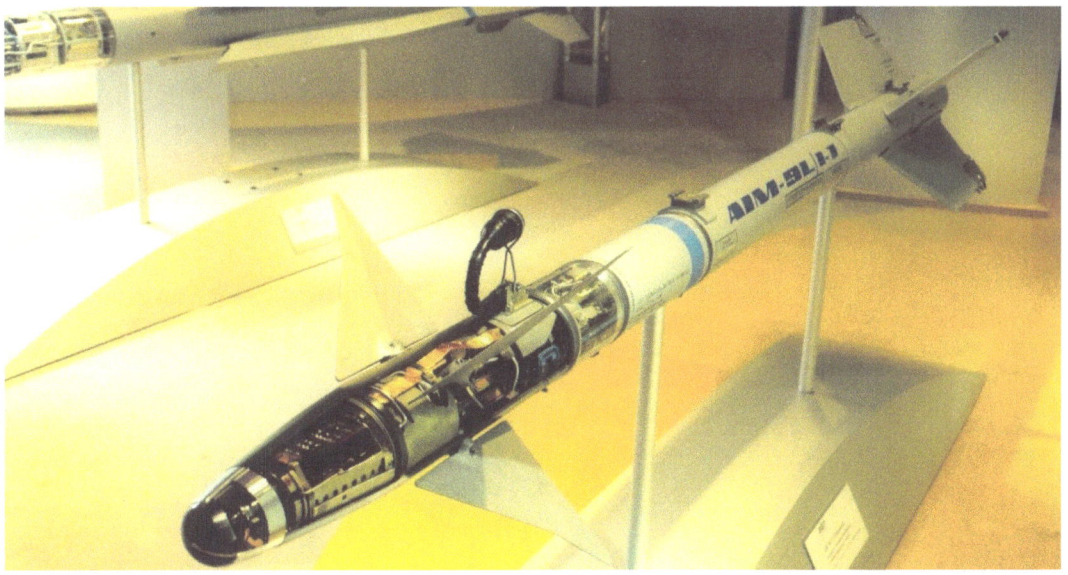

Proposed AIM-9L/1.1 update of the early 2000's. Author

ASRAAM was procured as a replacement for the legacy AIM-9L/M in RAF service under SR(A) 1234, primarily to arm the Panavia Tornado F.3 interceptor/air defence fighter (retired in 2011) and the Eurofighter Typhoon multirole strike fighter. Quasi-planning called for ASRAAM to be integrated on the Nimrod MRA4, although this would probably not have been followed up on following relaxation of the requirement for operations in a high threat environment.

The Ministry of Defence equipment policy committee had authorised ASRAAM development on 20 September 1990. Through a series of twists and turns, ASRAAM was selected to proceed to full-development and later serial production – prime contractor was BAe Dynamics (later MBDA (British Aerospace Dynamics Alenia). Prospects for ASRAAM to be developed as a NATO standard AIM-9 replacement under the AIM-132 designation effectively ended when the United States pursued an AIM-9L/M replacement program, which spawned the Raytheon AIM-9X Evolved Sidewinder.

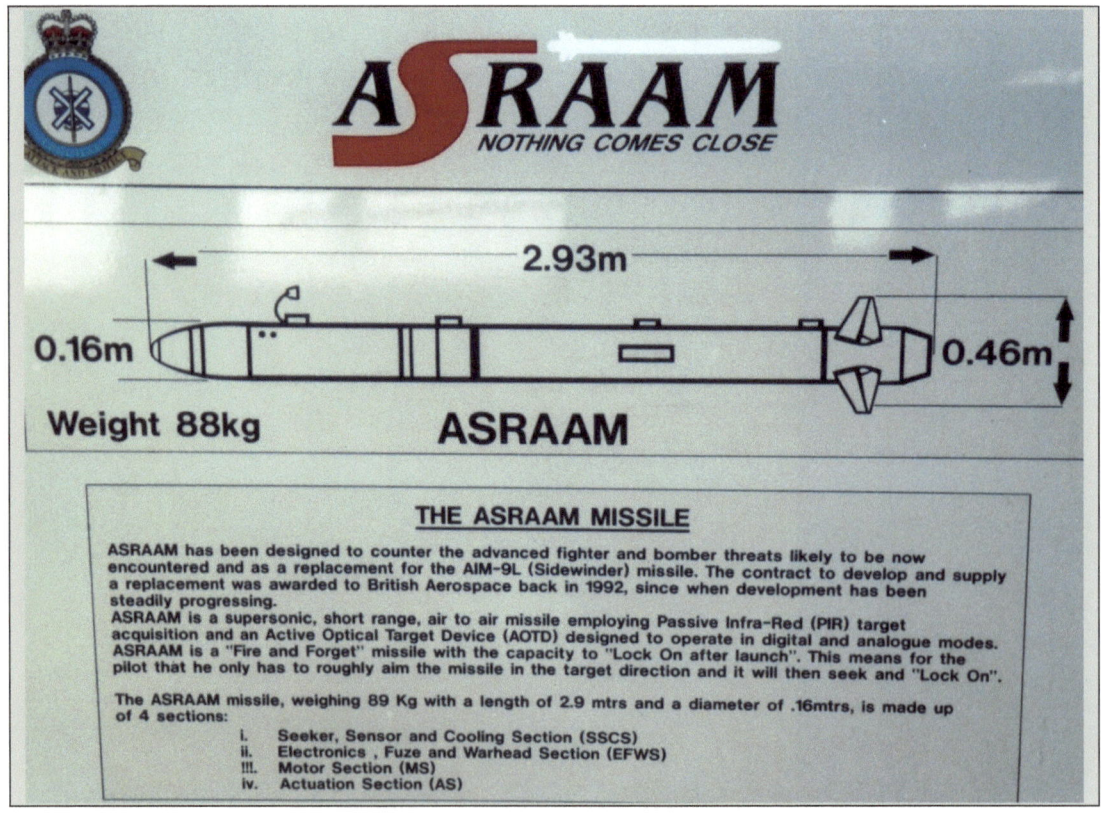

ASRAAM information sheet. Author

ASRAAM was made up of four sections: 1. SSCS (Seeker, Sensor and Cooling Section); 2. EFWS (Electronics Fuse and Warhead Section); MS (Motor Section) and AS (Actuation Section) (MoD RAF, 2004). At the cutting edge of short-range air to air missile technology, ASRAAM was designed as a highly agile, wingless, low drag missile, employing the combination of efficient power plant, body lift and rear aerodynamic control to achieve high performance and agility. Controlled by a software-driven autopilot, ASRAAM maintained high levels of agility throughout the missile flight, unlike thrust vector controlled missiles, which lose significant amount of energy through directing the thrust to manoeuvre the missile. Propulsion was provided by a Royal Ordnance smokeless (low signature) solid fuelled rocket motor, which accelerated the missile to multi-Mach speed – speed is classified, but was expected to be in the region of Mach 4/+. Initial speed would have been reduced slightly over that achievable by launch from a high performance tactical combat aircraft due to the Nimrod launch platform lower speed, which translated into lower launch energy and reduced velocity for the missile in the initial stage of flight (MBDA, Harkins, 2013).

ASRAAM training round of the RAF Leuchars Panavia Tornado F.3 Wing in 2004. Author

ASRAAM employed four small control fins at the rear of the body. The missile produced low levels of drag, contributing to its extended engagement range in relation to legacy systems and most international contemporaries. The long-range, which extended more or less out to the realm of beyond visual range (assuming a non-manoeuvring target approaching the launch platform) would have provided Nimrod MRA4 with a competent air to air capability against potential threats and would have provided the ability to intercept potential adversary maritime patrol aircraft over the sea/ocean in wartime conditions.

ASRAAM missile on the port outer wing station of a RAF Typhoon temporarily deployed to RAF Leuchars, Scotland, in September 2003. Author

From close range almost to beyond visual range, ASRAAM provisioned for all-round target designation with full acquisition anywhere in the forward hemisphere. Long range and short range target acquisition and track were facilitated by a Raytheon developed wide off-boresight gimballed 128x128 element focal plane array seeker and image processor. The seeker provided real-world imagery, extended acquisition range with unprecedented countermeasure resistance. Target destruction would be accomplished through actuation of the DASA (later EADS Germany) developed warhead by a Thorn EMI developed active infrared, laser proximity and or impact fuse Harkins, 2013).

RAF Tornado F.3 squadrons began training with the new missile in April 2002 and ASRAAM formed the IIR armament from delivery of the first RAF service Typhoons in 2002/2003 (training capacity) and formed the IIR air to air missile armament for UK F-35B Lightning II.

> ASRAAM – data furnished by MBDA
>
> Weight: 88 kg
> Length: 2.90 m
> Diameter: 0.166 m
> Warhead: Fragmentation
> Fuses: Laser proximity and impact
> Propulsion: Solid rocket motor
> Homing head: Imaging infrared 128x28 element focal plane array

BAE Systems Documentation highlighted that Nimrod MRA4 could carry up to four ALARM (2) (Air Launched Ant-Radiation Missiles) on the four main underwing stores stations, for use in an anti-radar role – such weapons home in on radiation emitted by radar systems. It is unclear if ALARM, which was in service with RAF Tornado tactical combat aircraft, would have been an armament option for the Nimrod MRA4 had it attained operational service.

ALARM, which was self-contained, operated against threat radar identified and located by the launch aircraft. Once launched, ALARM could zoom climb to an altitude in the region of ~21336 m (70,000 ft.) followed by a slow descent after deployment of a retarding parachute system – the missile onboard systems watching for a threat radar system to activate, after which it would be attacked. ALARM had an internal memory, which informed the missile guidance of target location after it had stopped transmitting. This mode of attack could be inaccurate.

MBDA ALARM anti-radiation missile aerodynamic shape alongside an ASRAAM aerodynamic shape. Author

Non-weapon stores options included: 5x3 Air Sea Rescue, or 5x3 dinghies, or 12 x survival containers or 36 x light series stores, carried in the internal stores bay (BAE, 2002).

Basic Performance – The Nimrod MRA4 had a maximum speed of Mach 0.77 and service ceiling was 12800 m (42,000 ft.) (BAE), allowing high speed transit to a patrol area over rough weather. Unrefuelled range was in excess of 11000 km (~5935 nm (UK)) with an endurance in excess of 14 hours (BAE). Conflicting BAE documentation states an endurance in excess of 15 hours. The increase in range over its predecessor was accomplished through a combination of higher fuel load carried, compared to that accommodated on the Nimrod MR2, and lower specific fuel burn per kilogram force thrust for the BR710 engines over the previous generation Rolls Royce Spey engines installed in the Nimrod MR2 (BAE, 2004 & BAE, 2002a). Air to air refuelling capability was facilitated through the incorporation of a fixed in-flight refuelling probe located on the upper forward fuselage (this was a refurbished inflight refuelling system carried over from the Nimrod MR2). The Nimrod MRA4 range/endurance was restricted only by crew endurance when air to air refuelling was employed. The increased endurance would potentially have allowed the Nimrod MRA4 to remain on station twice as long as the Nimrod MR2 during a search and rescue operation, without in-flight refuelling being employed (Harkins, 2004).

The program acquisition included not only the aircraft, but a full integrated training system, incorporating flight simulators and implementation of build work at planned operating base(s) to accommodate operational aspects of the weapons system, including maintenance and training facilities. The Nimrod MRA4 training system was designed as a fully integrated ground based and flight based syllabus. This would include the use of computer courseware, simulators, all ultimately leading to aircraft flight training (BAE, 2002). The integrated logistics support was designed to reduce to a minimum the life-cycle costs of operation of the Nimrod MRA4 fleet and attain an aircraft availability rate at least equal to that of modern civil airliners, in excess of that achieved by legacy large multi-engine aircraft (BAE, 2002). The aircraft was designed for operations from advanced base areas and operations away from the main operating base and its associated infrastructure. Such remote operations, which would have been controlled from portable mission and ground support systems transported to a forward base, would have been omitted when faced with a high threat capability adversary.

Nimrod MRA4 PA02 (ZJ518). BAE Systems

There were twenty one serials numbers allocated to the original planned twenty one Nimrod 2000 (MRA4). Of these, ZJ516, ZJ518 and ZJ517 were allocated to PA01, PA02 and PA03 respectively. Two other Nimrod MRA4, PA04 and PA05, attained flight status prior to program cancellation, these being allocated the serials ZJ514 and ZJ515 respectively. The remaining serials, allocated to the aircraft still on order at the time of cancellation and those previously cancelled in the several rounds of unit reductions, were as follows: ZJ519 (PA06), ZJ520 (PA07), ZJ521 (PA08), ZJ522 (PA09), ZJ523 (PA10), ZJ524 (PA11), ZJ525 (PA12), ZJ526, ZJ527, ZJ528, ZJ529, ZJ530, ZJ531, ZJ532, ZJ533 and ZJ534. Based on a usage rate of 650 flying hours per year, Nimrod MRA4 aircraft could have attained a service life of 25 years (not allowing for high intensity operations against a peer adversary) (PPR, 23.7.2003).

BAE Systems Nimrod MRA4 – data furnished by BAE Systems

Powerplant: 4 x Rolls-Royce (Germany) BR710 non-afterburning turbofan engines
Length: ~38.63 m (126 ft. 9 in)
Height, overall: ~9.29 m (30 ft. 6 in.)
Wing span: ~38.71 m (127 ft.)
Wing Area: ~235.8 m² (2,538 ft.²)
Basic (operating) empty weight: ~51150 kg (112,766 lb.)
Maximum unrefuelled weight: ~58287 kg (128,500 lb.)
Maximum take-off weight: ~106217 kg (234,165 lb.)
Maximum internal useable fuel mass: ~48999 kg (108,029 lb.)
Maximum payload: In excess of ~5443 kg (12,000 lb.)
Service ceiling: ~12800 m (42,000 ft.)
Unrefuelled range: In excess of 11000 km (~5935 nm)
Endurance: In excess of 14 hours
Air to air refuelling capability: Range/endurance is restricted only by crew endurance when air to air refuelling is available
Max speed: Mach 0.77

3

DEVELOPMENT AND TEST TO CANCELLATION

The Nimrod MRA4 program was administered by the Nimrod Maritime Reconnaissance and Attack MK4 (MRA4) program team, with overall Project Capability administered by the Head of Deterrent and Underwater Capability (NAO, 2010). The development route called for the components of three stripped down Nimrod MR2 to be transferred to FRA (Flight Refuelling Aviation) in Bournemouth for refurbishment before they were returned to BAe (British Aerospace) Woodford for use in the Nimrod MRA4 build process. The first of the stripped down airframes was delivered to Flight Refuelling Aviation in February 1997, with the other two following later the same year – the airframes were taken from long-term storage (NR, 2009 & NAO MPR, 1997).

In 1997, the airframe preliminary design review had been planned for February 1998 and the maiden flight of the first development aircraft was then scheduled for late 1999. In late 1998, BAe revealed that it would not be able to meet its contractual commitments in the previously agreed timescale. This resulted in contract renegotiations, which led to a number of alterations, subsequently approved by the EAC (Equipment Approval Committee) in April 1999, the new contract being formalised in May that year. The delays associated with the program now called for the air vehicle critical design review in September 1999, maiden flight for the first development aircraft in December 2001, and formal delivery of the first service aircraft in August 2004 (NR, 2009 & NAO MPR, 1999). In the event, the design review was completed in February 2000, clearing the way for the development aircraft build and qualification phases (NAO MPR, 2001).

Almost from program inception, the Nimrod MRA4 (Nimrod 2000) (ZJ518/PA02 illustrated) followed a troubled pathway to its ultimate cancellation. BAE Systems

Formal usage of the term RMPA (Replacement Maritime Patrol Aircraft) was discontinued in 1999. Following contract renegotiations in May 1999, responsibility for build of the Nimrod MRA4 aircraft moved from FRA to BAE Systems Woodford in October that year (as noted in the previous chapter, BAe became the entity of BAE Systems when it merged with the Systems element of the Marconi Electronic Systems in 1999) (BAE, 2020, NAO MPR, 2001 & NAO MPR, 1999).

As noted in the 2009 Nimrod review, UK (United Kingdom) Ministry of Defence procurement programs were historically beset by cost overruns and in-service date delays (NR, 2009). Going into the twenty first century the Nimrod MRA4 was not to be immune to this chronic condition prevalent within UK defence equipment procurement. When the Nimrod MRA4 program completed the detailed design phase in February 2000, the projected maiden flight of the first of the three development aircraft had been rescheduled for June 2002, a delay of some six months over the previous estimate (NAO MPR, 2001). A routine program review in 2002 would ultimately lead to a reduction in the numbers of Nimrod MRA4 to be procured from 21 to 18. This would reduce program costs by £114 million (without taking into account other factors, which could alter this upward or downward) (NAO MPR, 2010). The program reduction from 21 to 18 aircraft was formally notified to Parliament on 28 February 2002. By the time of the 2002 (NAO MPR) National Audit Office Major Programs Report, the first flight for the first development Nimrod MRA4 was rescheduled to take place before the end of that year, with the second scheduled to fly by Spring 2003 (NAO MPR, 2002). The program continued to be beset with technical and procurement issues. A further program review led to a 19 February 2003 (NAO MPR, 2003 states 23 February) decision to move away from the previously agreed fixed price contract for aircraft design and development (NAO MPR, 2010 & PPR, 23.7.2003). Now the design and manufacturing areas of the program were, as far as was practicable, separated in a process for reducing risk prior to customer price and schedule commitment. This had the effect that only the three development aircraft were funded at this point – the contact had moved from fixed price to what was termed Target Cost Incentive Fee in regard to design and development. The option for fifteen serial aircraft would be funded after risk had been assessed and costing agreed (NAO MPR, 2004 & NAO MPR, 2003). Until such time as the series production standard Nimrod MRA4 had been clearly defined, no series production activity was to be undertaken, other than that which was related to ensuring the maintenance of contractor design skill base in order that said skills base was not allowed to critically evaporate, and to ensure the supply chain was preserved (NAO MPR, 2010 & PPR, 23.7.2003).

The delays emanating from the 2003 program reorganisation allowed time for reassessment of aircraft capability requirements, already complying with the North Atlantic Treaty Organisation Defence Capabilities Initiative, through a concept study, followed by an assessment study then scheduled to commence in autumn 2003. This would also explore the Nimrod MRA4 platform potential for contribution to the wider network centricity, increasing the operational potential of all linked assets (PPR, 23.7.2003). The SDR (Strategic Defence Review) New Chapter identified a potential requirement for increased capability in reconnaissance, surveillance and land attack capability. This would result in a study into the potential for adapting the program to include increased capability in those areas. Additional to these studies was the identification of the potential for future development of the program to incorporate ISTAR (Intelligence Surveillance Target Acquisition and Reconnaissance) and deep strike capabilities – ISTAR entered the equation as a potential mission role for the MRA4 in the 2003/2004 timeframe (NAO, 2010, NAO MPR, 2004 & PPR, 23.7.2003).

The post February 2003 schedule called for the maiden flight of the first development aircraft by June 2004, the second development aircraft to fly by August that year and the third development aircraft to fly by mid-2005. The first service aircraft delivery was scheduled for late 2007, with an in-service date of early 2009 and final service capability delivery (the sixth serial aircraft) in 2011. The now scheduled in-service date of 2009 was expected to be difficult to achieve (NAO MPR, 2004, NAO MPR, 2003 & PPR, 23.7.2003). Under the eighteen Nimrod MRA4 requirement, seventeen were to be available for operations and a single aircraft would be held as a fleet sustainment unit to cover when an aircraft was in deep maintenance or as an attrition replacement. All, including the fleet sustainment unit, were to be available for operations within 60 days (PPR, 23.7.2003).

In July 2004, a study was conducted to determine the number of Nimrod MRA4 airframes that would be required to ensure the United Kingdom could continue to meet its requirement for maritime patrol/reconnaissance (NAO, 2010 & NAO MPR, 2004). This number was set at twelve airframes, a reduction in six from the eighteen MRA4 (3 development and options on 15 series) covered by the modified contract of February 2003, and a reduction in nine from the original contract covering twenty one airframes. The conclusions of the study led to a formal reduction of overall Nimrod MRA4 from eighteen to twelve, formally announced in July 2004. At this time it was confirmed that the RAF (Royal Air Force) was operating an active fleet of twenty one Nimrod MR2 (NAO MRP, 2004a). The reduction by one third in unit numbers to be procured was estimated to reduce program costs by £155 million (without taking into account other factors, which could alter this upward or downward) (NAO, 2010). Another review highlighted additional program cost concerns, pre-existing and potentially exacerbated by the further reduction in aircraft numbers to be acquired. Increased costing associated with production would require the entry to service date for the Nimrod MRA4 to be further delayed in order to address affordability issues amid funding constraints.

The prototype Nimrod MRA4, PA01 (ZJ516). BAE Systems

As noted above, in 2001, first Nimrod MRA4 development aircraft maiden flight was not expected until June 2002, around six months later than the date agreed in the renegotiated contractual obligations of 1999. The then projected in-service date of 2005 was expected to suffer another delay (NAO, 2001). As a result, studies were conducted to mitigate against capability shortfalls by potentially introducing incremental capability enhancements to the extant Nimrod MR2 fleet. This would be accomplished primarily through the RAP (Replacement Acoustic Processor) program, through which processors for the AQS 971 installed in the Nimrod MR2 would be replaced by processors developed for the AQS 970 acoustic complex of the Nimrod MRA4 (in 2001). In addition, the navigation, communications and datalink systems would be updated (in 2002), benefiting from technology planned for the Nimrod MRA4 fleet (NR, 2009, NAO MPR, 2004, NAO MPR, 2003, NAO MPR, 2002 & NAO MPR, 2001).

The necessity to keep the Nimrod MR2 fleet in service longer than planned led to an expansion of the AAA (Ageing Aircraft Audit) remit to address Nimrod systems being retained in service longer than planned – previously the AAA had evaluated Nimrod structures from 1993 and again in a review of 2003 (NR, 2009). The ageing airframes dictated the planned out of service dates of 2006 and 2009 for the Nimrod MR2 and Nimrod R1 respectively – electronic surveillance capability provided by the Nimrod R1 was to be carried on through Project Helix (NAO MPR, 2009), met through acquisition of second hand Boeing RC-135 electronic surveillance aircraft surplus to United States Air Force requirements. Operational demands for use in Afghanistan and delays to the in-service date of the Nimrod MRA4 would be attributed as contributing causes that led to the accidental loss of Nimrod MR2 XV277 over Afghanistan in 2006 – under original Nimrod MRA4 in-service date planning, this aircraft would have been retired prior to the date it was lost (NR, 2009).

In the February 2003 program alterations, the Nimrod MRA4 in-service date was moved to March 2009, this later being pushed out to September 2009 (NAO MPR, 2004). This would reflect on the Nimrod MR2 out of service date, which would now be delayed until March 2011 (NR, 2009). This, although some five years beyond the MR2 out of service date of 2006 advocated by the AAA, was now considered the time required for sufficient Nimrod MRA4 aircraft to be operational to adequately replace the tasking's of the Nimrod MR2 fleet.

The 2005 NAO MPR pushed the Nimrod MRA4 in-service date to 2010. Lack of funding led to the uncertainty as to whether or not this would result in a capability loss between Nimrod MR2 scheduled out of service date of March 2011 and sufficient numbers of Nimrod MRA4 being available, or whether the Nimrod MR2 out of service date would be extended yet again. This uncertainty was not addressed in the 2006 and 2007 NAO MPR, which held no change for Nimrod MRA4 in-service date. The 2008 NAO MRP confirmed a further delay of three months to the Nimrod MRA4 in-service date. By this time the program was in excess of ten years late in regard to in-service date and some £789 million over the original cost forecast (NR, 2009).

Amid the program changes being implemented to address cost and other problems, the contractor was pushing ahead with preparations for commencement of flight test of PA01, the first of the three Nimrod MRA4 prototype/development aircraft. The flight test phase would formally commence when PA01 conducted its maiden flight from BAE Systems Woodford facility on 26 August 2004, landing at BAE Systems Warton facility (NAO, 2010, BAE, 2004 & Harkins, 2004). The second development aircraft, PA02, conducted its maiden flight on 15 December 2004. On 20 December that year, in response to questions in

Parliament, the UK Defence Minister confirmed that the entry to service date was then projected for 2009 (Parliament, 2004).

Nimrod MRA4 PA01 (ZJ516) raises its nose during high speed taxi trials. BAE Systems

Flight Test, 2004-2005 – Flight Testing of the Nimrod MRA4 aircraft was conducted under the auspices of a JTT (Joint Trials Team), consisting of BAE Systems, the DRA (Defence Procurement Agency), the RAF and Qinetic. As noted above, the contract amendments agreed in February 2003 had called for the first three Nimrod MRA4 – PA01, PA02 and PA03 – to be built and released as development aircraft to conduct the ambitious flight test program. The success or failure of this would determine whether or not serial production would be authorised (BAE Gill & Bellamy, 2005). PA01 was to be employed primarily as an air test vehicle to assess handling characteristics, conduct flutter, stall and general systems trials and push out flight envelope expansion. For its trials role, PA01, which lacked most of the mission systems planned for the serial Nimrod MRA4, was equipped with an extensive instrumentation suite and a battery of work stations for a crew of test/trials observers. PA02 was primarily tasked with mission system trials, for which it was equipped with the development missions systems intended for serial production. PA02 was also tasked with conducting environmental trials for operation in hot and cold climates and for stores carriage and separation trials. PA03 was primarily tasked with testing the avionics elements of the mission systems, navigation suite, Automatic Flight Control System, and clearance of the Defensive Aids Sub-System and the Electronic Sensor Measures suite for operation from serial aircraft. PA03 was also tasked with assessing the noise environment and vibration levels in the crew compartments during flight operations (BAE Gill & Bellamy, 2005).

Prior to PA01's maiden flight, a series of low and high speed taxi trials were conducted at Woodford. Low speed braking was conducted on 12 and 13 June 2004. In regard to the braking system, data was garnered from trials with the iron bird (ground test rig) as the ground run phase of aircraft flight tests was considered an engineering issue rather than flight test issue, despite being organised by the Flight Test Engineering department. On 9 July 2004, acceleration and braking trials were conducted at speeds below ~130 km/h (70 knots). On 21, 23 and 24 August 2004, braking from high speed was trialed. On 25 August 2004, the eve of PA01's maiden flight, the nose was raised during a taxi run in order to test compatibility of the air intake design (BAE Gill & Bellamy, 2005).

As briefly recounted above, PA01 conducted a maiden flight on 26 August 2004. The Aircraft moved into position to initiate the take-off run from Runway 25 at BAE Systems Woodford at 14.31 hours (crew consisted of BAE Systems Chief Test Pilot, John Turner (crew Captain); Bill Oval (Co-Pilot); Paul Bayley (FTO) and Harry Nockolds (Mission Crew-Cabin Safety). Once airborne, PA01 flew for 1 hour, 56 minutes (a Pilatus PC-9 and a BAE Systems Hawk T.1 were employed as chase aircraft to accompany PA01 on the maiden flight), during which it assessed a number of test areas: handling at low airspeeds; calibration of the on-board air data system with that of a chase aircraft; engagement and assessment of yaw damping; the full spectrum of wing flap cycling; retraction and deployment of the undercarriage; preliminary assessment of lateral and direction handling characteristics; preliminary assessment of longitudinal static stability and preliminary handling assessment of the BR701 engines, including sudden acceleration and deceleration. Data from flight instrumentation was relayed by data-link to ground stations at Woodford and Warton, where the aircraft landed on Runway 26 at the conclusion of the flight (BAE Gill & Bellamy, 2005).

Nimrod MRA4 PA01 conducted a maiden flight from BAE Woodford on 26 August 2004. BAE Systems

The flight confirmed computational/simulator pre-flight predictions in regard to aircraft handling. A number of minor issues were uncovered for fix: there had been an un-authorised premature rotation during the take-off run; both radio altimeters suffered in-flight failures; a few anomalous caution/warning indications were received and higher than anticipated elevator 'trimmer gearing' was encountered (BAE Gill & Bellamy, 2005).

On the 26 August 2004 maiden flight, PA01 flew in company with a Pilatus PC-9 and BAE Hawk chase aircraft. BAE Systems

Following PA01's maiden flight, the aircraft was grounded for modifications, including to the braking system and FCS (Flight Control System)/cockpit display standard, which was updated to software version L4.2, intended to reduce flight crew workload (the maiden flight had been conducted with the display standard employed in the pre-maiden flight ground test phase) (BAE Gill & Bellamy, 2005).

The eighth taxi trial was conducted on 13 October 2004, during which the modified braking system was evaluated to clear the aircraft for its second flight, which was conducted on 15 October that year. This flight, which lasted 2 hours, 13 minutes, provided evaluation data on the functionality of the modified FCS. The third flight, conducted on 1

November 2004, lasted 1 hour, 26 minutes, during which the aircraft conducted low flyby's over the airfield and conducted air data calibration. The fourth flight, conducted on 4 November 2004, had a duration of 2 hours, 34 minutes, during which the aircraft general handling and operation of the Identification Friend or Foe Mode C was assessed (BAE Gill & Bellamy, 2005).

The ninth taxy trial was conducted on 19 November 2004, during which modification introduced to the braking system was evaluated to clear the aircraft for its fifth flight, which was conducted on 25 November that year. This flight, which had a duration of 2 hours, 1 minute, involved assessing general handling and anti-ice dry air testing (BAE Gill & Bellamy, 2005).

The enlarged wing nacelles of the Nimrod MRA4 are shown prominently in this view of PA01 during the early trials phase. BAE Systems

Following the 25 November 2004 flight, PA01 would not fly again for several months. The focus of runway and flight testing would now fall upon PA02, which commenced low speed taxi trials – included assessing the operation of the nose wheel steering – on 8 December 2004, followed by high speed brake trials on the 9th and high speed brake and nose raising trials on the 10th, in order to assess the efficiency of the air intake system. The taxi trials paved the way for the maiden flight of PA02, which, as recounted above, was conducted on 15 December 2004, in a flight of 2 hours, 4 minutes duration. This milestone attained the business objective calling for the first two development aircraft to fly before the end of 2004 (BAE Gill & Bellamy, 2005).

On 21 December 2004, PA02 conducted its second flight and the last Nimrod MRA4 flight of 2004. Flight duration was 1 hour, 26 minutes, during which general handling characteristics were assessed. Radio navigation trials were conducted on PA02's 2 hour, 3 minute duration third flight, conducted on 13 January 2005, followed by the fourth flight, conducted on 8 February 2005. This flight, of 3 hours, 7 minutes duration, assessed handling characteristics. Searchwater 2000MR radar testing commenced on PA02's fifth flight, of 2 hour, 25 minute duration, conducted on 10 February 2005. PA02's sixth flight, of 2 hour, 54 minutes duration, which was conducted on 17 February 2005, tested approach aids. The next two flights, of 2 hours, 33 minutes (conducted on 21 February 2005) and 3 hours, 3 minutes (conducted on 25 February 2005) duration respectively, were focused primarily on assessing the radio navigation aids. General handling assessment was the main focus of PA02's ninth flight, of 2 hours, 31 minutes duration, which was conducted on 1 March 2005. Searchwater 2000MR radar functionality tests and assessment of the Environmental Control System were conducted on PA02's 3 hour, 48 minute duration tenth flight, which was conducted on 3 March 2005. This was followed by two general handling characteristic flight tests of 2 hours (conducted on 14 April 2005) and 2 hours, 7 minutes (conducted on 19 April 2005) respectively. Flights

thirteen (2 hours, 47 minutes duration) and flight fourteen (2 hours, 19 minutes duration) of PA02, focused on assessment of the radio navigation aids/autonomous navigation capability and radio navigation aids respectively (BAE Gill & Bellamy, 2005).

Previous page and above: PA02 (ZJ518) conducted a maiden flight on 15 December 2004. BAE Systems

During its grounding, PA01 had been employed on ground resonance testing – conducted from November 2004 into February 2005. The aircraft returned to flight test tasking's when it took to the air in a 3 hour, 47 minute duration flight conducted on 29 April 2005. This flight, PA01's sixth and the twentieth Nimrod MRA4 flight overall, focused primarily on trials concerning engine relights. PA01 continued flight tests on 4 May 2005 when it took off on a 57 minute duration flight, during the course of which deceleration and fuel dumping trials were conducted (BAE Gill & Bellamy, 2005).

Around the time of PA01's return to flight testing, PA03 had been undergoing preparation for ground test, including engine runs, that would lead to a 75 minute maiden flight from Woodford (apparently conducted on 29 December 2005) (PPR Session, 2010-11, 2011 & BAE Gill & Bellamy, 2005).

Nimrod MRA4 PA02 takes off to fly across the Atlantic Ocean to Florida, USA, for environmental trials, circa 26 September 2006. BAE Systems

PA01, which was not equipped with mission systems, continued to be employed on airframe/engine testing until 2009. PA02 continued mission system test flights and deployments for climatic tests and conducted an airfield performance phase at McKinley Climatic Facility, Eglin Air Force Base, Florida, USA, and Istres air base, France, respectively. By the time of the program cancellation in late 2010, PA02 had conducted in excess of 230 flights. PA03, which continued to be operated on mission system flight development, had conducted in excess of 60 flights by the time of the programs cancellation (PPR Session 2010-11, 2011).

Business approval for reintroducing the production requirement had been formally granted in May 2006, with the serial production requirement formally reintroduced in a contract amendment dated July 2006. This process had included affirmation by the Investment Approval Board of key requirements, by then termed KUR (Key User Requirements): 01. Maritime Counter Terrorism; 02. Search & Detect (UWE); 03. Submarine Attack; 04. Search & Detect (AWE); 05. Tactical Interoperability; 06. Mission Completion; 07. Maritime Presence; 08.

Operations in Hostile Environment (at this stage of the program this requirement was at risk of not being incorporated as it was no longer considered an operational requirement for the post 2010 period (NAO MPR, 2009)) and 09. Environmental Operating Conditions (NAO MPR Vol. II, 2007). Into 2008, all but three of the KUR –Tactical Interoperability, Maritime Presence and Environmental Operating Conditions – were at risk of not being met, the Maritime Presence also falling into this category going into 2009 (NAO MPR, 2009 & NAO MPR PS, 2008).

Nimrod MRA4 PA02 during environmental testing at the McKinley Climatic Laboratory, Eglin air force base, Florida, USA. The aircraft was tested to environmental conditions of -40 Centigrade. BAE Systems

The authorisation for series production resulted in further amendments to the development/production contract, including acceptance of what was termed Key Performance Measures and a revision of planned entry to service date (NAO MPR, 2010). This resulted in a production contract for twelve series production Nimrod MRA4 aircraft being confirmed by the Minister for Defence on 18 July 2006. The Defence minister confirmed that the three flying development aircraft had induced confidence that the program had matured to a point where production could be authorised. Acknowledging that the program had been plagued by schedule and cost overruns, the Minister emphatically stated that these had been stabilised through the various restructuring measures implemented since February 2003 (Parliament, 2006).

The first serial produced Nimrod MRA4, PA04 (ZJ514), conducted a maiden flight on 10 September 2009. This aircraft was delivered to the RAF on 19 March 2010, but apparently continued to be flown by the BAE Systems test team crew at the time of program cancellation. The last of the Nimrod MRA4's to attain flight status was PA05 (ZJ515), which had conducted a maiden flight on 8 March 2010, the program being cancelled just some six months later.

The first serial produced Nimrod MRA4, PA04 (ZJ514), painted in RAF service livery on 10 November 2009. BAE Systems

The program had continued to beset by financial concerns, affordability issues having arisen again in spring 2008, leading directly to yet another reduction in the number of aircraft to be procured – this was reduced from 12 to 9 (NAO MPR, 2010), falling below the number previously identified as that required to retain a viable maritime patrol capability post withdrawal of the Nimrod MR2 from operational service.

While the writing was not quite on the wall for the Nimrod MRA4 program just yet, the program suffered another setback in December 2009, with the announcement by the Secretary of State for Defence that in-service date would be further delayed as the Ministry of Defence embarked upon measures 'reprioritising defence expenditure to focus on current operations' (NAO MPR, 2010). The Nimrod MRA4 program was now becoming a financial casualty of the British operation in Afghanistan. The irony of this was that an operation against insurgent Taliban touted by the political establishment as necessary to contribute to Britain's security, had the net effect that it was compromising that very security by delaying, even threatening cancellation of, an asset fundamentally essential to preserving the United Kingdom's strategic nuclear deterrent, and ensuring control of her sea lanes and littoral waters in peace time, or in the eventuality of a war with a major power (Harkins, letter to Gov., 2010). A 22 month delay was pushed with a new entry to service date set for October 2012 (NAO MPR, 2010).

Following the introduction of serial aircraft to flight status, the development aircraft retained the lion's share of the burden to clear the aircraft/systems. This Nimrod MRA4 is hooked up to ground power during ground operations – note the open stores bay doors – with the tail section of the first Nimrod MRA4 development aircraft, PA01, in the background. BAE Systems

Operational Capability – The initial requirement for declaring an IOC (Initial Operational Capability) with the Nimrod MRA4 had been delivery of the seventh serial produced aircraft to the RAF. This was changed in accordance with MPR04 Definition (authorised in the 19 February 2003 program changes, which reduced from 21 to 18 the number of aircraft to be procured). Operational capability was now considered to be contingent on delivery of the sixth serial aircraft as it was decreed that there would be six aircraft allocated to each operational squadron. MPR07 Definition resulted in a change to IOC being contingent on delivery of five aircraft (only 4 for deployment) and six trained aircrews. This was in accordance with changes announced in July 2004, for a reduction in Nimrod MRA4 numbers to be procured from 18 to 12. MPR09 called for IOC to be contingent on delivery of four Nimrod MRA4, with only four available trained aircrews. This change, which effectively removed the non-deployable aircraft from the IOC requirement, was in line with the program reduction from 12 to 9 aircraft. The 2010 Definition for IOC was MPR10, which required delivery of five Nimrod MRA4, with six trained aircrews, to facilitate the capability to conduct a standing patrol of one aircraft, sustained for a period of seven days (NAO MPR, 2010).

The change to an IOC of October 2012 (a 114 month slippage from the original in-service estimate of April 2003) indicated that a gap in operational maritime reconnaissance capability was unavoidable if the Nimrod MR2 out of service date of March 2010 was to be met (the MR2 was retired on 31 March 2010) (NAO MPR, 2010). Running on the remaining Nimrod MR2 fleet would have been fraught with difficulties due to corrosion problems and other fuel leak issues. As far back as 2007, the United Kingdom government had confirmed that over the period 1 October 2006 to 31 March 2007, the Nimrod MR2 and Nimrod R1 fleets had suffered no less than 25 fuel leaks. There were then no in place plans for refurbishment of the Nimrod MR2 fleet before replacement by the Nimrod MRA4 (Hansard, 2007).

To partially offset the capability loss from retirement of the Nimrod MR2 fleet prior to the planned operational capability with the Nimrod MRA4, it was decreed that Royal Navy Merlin MK1 helicopters and RAF Lockheed Hercules transport aircraft would be employed on ersatz maritime patrol/reconnaissance duties. These assets were unsuited, nor properly equipped for these tasks, therefore, it was further decreed that a limited capability could be afforded by whatever Nimrod MRA4 aircraft were available prior to full IOC being attained (NAO MPR, 2010). As noted above, deliveries of Nimrod MRA4 to the intended operator had commenced in March 2010 (although still under contractor operation), the entry-to-service date being reaffirmed as October 2012 on 16 June that year – a limited capability was to be made available prior to the full entry to service (Hansard, 16 June 2010).

The clearance for RAF crews to operate the Nimrod MRA4 was conducted under the MAA (Military Aviation Authority), a new entity for which the Nimrod MRA4 program was the first to go through. At the time of program cancellation in October 2010, the MAA clearance for RAF operation of the Nimrod MRA4 had not been completed (PPR Session 2010-11, 2011).

Nimrod MRA4 during a development flight over the Arctic. BAE Systems

In late 2010 (a new government had taken office in May 2010), a reaffirmation to the program requirement pointed to adverse effects that would result in the eventuality that the program was cancelled. Foremost among these was the fact that the strategic nuclear deterrent, present in the Trident SLBM (Submarine Launched Ballistic Missile) armed Vanguard SSBN (Nuclear Powered Ballistic Missile Submarine) fleet, operating out of Faslane Naval Base in Western Scotland, would not be sufficiently protected. The protection of UK Sovereignty from potential air or maritime intrusions into UK airspace/territorial waters would be compromised (NAO, 2010) and a number of civil tasking, such as search and rescue, would not be available. Appeals to keep the Nimrod MRA4 program alive were to no avail, the new Conservative government announcing the programs cancellation in the 2010 defence review – at this time the program was in the Post Main Investment Phase (NAO MPR, 2010). It was confirmed that the reasoning behind the decision to cancel the Nimrod MRA4 program was that it was estimated to save the Ministry of Defence around £2 billion over a ten year period (Parliament, 2011). What was not revealed at that time was whether or not this figure included the settlement to the contractors (this was withheld from public disclosure), but disposal of the Nimrod aircraft cost a stated further £200 million, reducing the estimated cost savings to £1.8 billion over ten years. Of course, the cost savings were completely undone and more with the inevitable ordering of a replacement for the Nimrod MRA4 to reintroduce a capability that was essential to the security of the United Kingdom – Boeing P-8 Poseidon maritime patrol aircraft were ordered directly from the United States at a cost of ~£3 billion, these not coming into service until 2020.

PA02 just inland from the Welsh coast. BAE Systems

A number of reasons were cited for the program cancellation, technical issues, cost and in-service date delays. When the main investment decision had been initiated, program cost was estimated at £2,183 million. The forecast cost of the Nimrod MRA4 program at 31 March 2010 was put at £3,602 million, an increase of £1,189 million (this actually represented an in-year cost variation of -£45 million) (NAO, 2010). By contrast, the two Queen Elizabeth Class aircraft carriers ordered for the British Royal Navy were costed at £4,085 million at main investment decision with a 31 March 2010 cost projection increased to £5,900 million, an increase of £1,815 million (actually represented an in-year cost variation of £767 million) (NAO, 2010).

That the program was tethering on the brink was evident prior to 2010, with the decision taken not to convert the three development aircraft to series production standard, along with extending flight testing/trials, which resulted in multi-million pound program costs savings. However, much of the cost savings would be offset due to costs of corrosion in a number of donor parts from the Nimrod MR2 fleet. In 2010, a further £110 million was withdrawn from Nimrod MRA4 program funding and allocated to other defence expenditure areas (NAO MPR, 2010).

There is no doubt that the Nimrod MRA4 program had been bedeviled by a number of development problems, many of which had been overcome or had fixes in the works when the program was cancelled. While it was clear from the earliest days following cancellation that cost was the overriding reason, media hype would shine the spotlight on other contributing factors, some of which were unwarranted criticism. For example, claims that there were safety issues in opening the stores bay doors and problems with the undercarriage during retraction or deployment appear to be unwarranted. The best available information from the development team and government departments indicate that there was no problems associated with operation of the stores bay doors and that there were no instances when the undercarriage failed to retract or deploy. In regard to the latter issue, two incidents were noted in which nose wheel indicators failed. The faults were identified and corrected. Another claim concerned the engines overheating during flight tests with one or more of the aircraft. The test team confirmed that there were no actual incidents in which the engines were subjected to overheat (PPR Session 2010-11, 2011). It should be born in mind that the engine technology had been tried, tested and operated in other aircraft platforms for around a decade and a half prior to the Nimrod MRA4 cancellation. Another concern noted in the media was that the Nimrod MRA4 was limited in its ability to operate in cold (ice) conditions. It is certainly fact that the fleet extant in 2010 had such limitations. However, this was due to the fact that testing had not been completed by the Qinetic test team and further operating clearances would have been expected once this testing had run its course (PPR Session 2010-11, 2011).

Nimrod MRA4 over the Welsh coast. BAE Systems

Significant faults that were in actuality included gaps discovered in the engine walls and a small area of vulnerability to foreign object damage (bird strike) in flight. The gap identified between the aircraft structure and engine bay fire wall had been addressed by a temporary fix and later eradicated through a permanent fix prior to program cancellation. The vulnerability to bird strike concerned a small area of ~15.24 cm x ~10.1 cm (6 inch x 4 inch) located in the internal stores bay. The concern was that a foreign object entering the open stores bay could impact this area and have a detrimental effect on the aircraft aileron control. This vulnerability was apparently eliminated through introduction of a cover over the affected area (PPR Session 2010-11, 2011).

Nimrod MRA4, PA04 (ZJ514). BAE Systems

One argument put forward to justify cancellation of the program was that as unit numbers to be procured had been cut by 57%, unit costs had risen by 199% (projected at £266 million per aircraft (this was an unconfirmed estimate). Among the most compelling evidence that the program cancellation was fiscal minded (in excess of £3.6 billion had been spent on the program at the time of cancellation) rather than technical was evident from the 2010 Strategic Defence Review which stated:

> "The October 2010 Strategic Defence and Security Review had a number of consequences for the Departments equipment program. A key issue was to address the long-term imbalance between anticipated Defence budget and forecast expenditure. To address this challenge the Department cancelled the Nimrod maritime patrol aircraft and also delayed introducing the Successor nuclear-deterrent submarine by four years to 2028" (NAO MPR, 2010 & NR, 2009).

In the end, the reasons were academic to the ultimate fate of the Nimrod program, which was sealed when the Nimrod MRA4 airframes were scrapped at BAE Woodford (PA04 was apparently scrapped at Warton) in a rushed through process during January-March 2011. The hast in which the airframes were scrapped was a clear indication that the government was ensuring the program could not be resurrected following a review process.

With the demise of the Nimrod MRA4 program a makeshift capability was required to reduce the vulnerability gaps in Britain's defence. As had been the case with plans to plug capability gaps between Nimrod MR2 retirement and Nimrod MRA4 in-service date the, Merlin helicopter, in-service with the Royal Navy, and Hercules transport aircraft, in service with the RAF, were put forward. The Nimrod MRA4 ISTAR/ELINT (Electronic Intelligence) function overland was not available in either the Merlin or Hercules (PPR, 23.7.2003) – this capability was to be sourced as a dedicated asset. While the Hercules had no anti-submarine warfare capability, Merlin could conduct this mission at short range, out to ~370 km (200 nm), for 90 minute duration. This was a significant reduction on the 11000 km (~5935 nm) range/14 hour endurance offered by the Nimrod MRA4. While Nimrod MRA4 surface vessel surveillance could be conducted at ~667 km (360 nm) at ~12192 m (40,000 ft.) altitude, the Merlin could conduct surface vessel surveillance only at limited range and at significantly lower altitudes with limited sensor capability. The Hercules could extend this range, but with no effective sensor capability. Nimrod MRA4 could provide fleet protection duties at enhanced range over that of the Merlin – the Hercules could not provide a fleet protection function (PPR Session 2010-11, 2011). The search and rescue capability offered by Nimrod MRA4, out to a range of ~4448 km (2400 nm) with a 3 hour search/loiter, was considerably in excess of the 1 hour loiter/search at ~556 km (300 nm) capability of the Merlin or the very limited sensor capability at ~1112 km (600 nm) range, with a 2 hour loiter/search, available with the Hercules (PPR Session 2010-11, 2011). Whilst the Hercules could provision the emergency communications capability incorporated in the Nimrod MRA4 (this was absent in the Merlin), it could not conduct a forward deployed maritime patrol capability or anti-piracy patrols, these capabilities being absent in the Merlin also. Hercules could not provide the required protection to the nuclear deterrent Trident ballistic missile submarine operations or protect future planned carrier task groups (such task groups would not be available until the aircraft carrier HMS *Queen Elizabeth* commissioned into the Royal Navy some years after the cancellation of the Nimrod MRA4 program). While the Merlin could provide limited protection to Trident submarines, this capability was at significantly reduced range in comparison to that offered by the Nimrod MRA4 (PPR Session 2010-11, 2011).

The limited short-range anti-submarine/maritime patrol capability offered by the Royal Navy Merlin MK1 helicopter was inadequate to replace the capability offered by Nimrod MRA4. Crown Copyright

From retirement of the Nimrod MR2 at the end of March 2010, the UK maritime patrol tasking fell upon the Merlin and Hercules. The lack of capability offered by these platforms was felt immediately, leading to the decision to procure a new maritime patrol platform to fill the capability gap left by retirement of Nimrod MR2 and cancellation of Nimrod MRA4. There was no solution to this that could be filled by a British prime contractor as the government had ordered the accelerated destruction of the Nimrod airframes, noted above. This left a foreign airframe solution as the only way forward.

During the development phase, Nimrod MRA4 had little real export prospects. BAE Systems had been involved in the US MMA (Multi Mission Aircraft) CAD Phase 1, but withdrew from this in 2002 (PPR, 23.7.2003). In a twist of fate, rather than the unlikely selection of the Nimrod MRA4 for the US MMA, which had led to development launch of the P-8A Poseidon (Boeing 737 passenger airliner derived) in 2004, the P-8 would, as the Poseidon MRA1, eventually fill the void left by the cancellation of the Nimrod MRA4 program in RAF service.

Another anti-submarine warfare asset touted as partially replacing the Nimrod fleet mission by partnering the Merlin helicopters, was the small force of Royal Navy Type 23 Frigate's, which, in actuality, could not take on any mission capability lost with the demise of the Nimrod fleet. GKN Westland

Nimrod MRA4/P-8 (Poseidon MRA1) basic comparison – The P-8 range of ~7413 km (4,000 nm) was one third less than the ~11000 km (~5935 nm) range of the Nimrod MRA4 and the P-8 endurance was in the region of 4 hours less than that of the Nimrod MRA4. The P-8 service ceiling of ~12497 m (41,000 ft.) was ~305 m (1,000 ft.) below the 12800 m (42,000 ft.) ceiling of the Nimrod MRA4 (Boeing, BAE, RAF). The area of basic performance that the P-8 was in advance of the Nimrod MRA4 was in maximum speed. This was set at Mach 0.82 (Boeing), 490 knots (907 km/h) (RAF), against Mach 0.77 for the Nimrod MRA4 (BAE). Maximum payload, at ~9072 kg (20,000 lb.) (RAF) for the P-8, was greater than the in excess of 5443 kg (12,000 lb.)

of the Nimrod MRA4 (BAE). The higher payload of the P-8 did not necessarily translate into increased combat persistence as the Nimrod MRA4 could carry more than twice as many torpedoes (9) as the P-8 (4) (Boeing & BAE) – the P-8 was equipped with US weapons, cementing the complete off the shelf purchase of the America system – the Sting Ray Mod 1 acquisition program had been terminated when the Nimrod MRA4 was cancelled in 2010.

Previous page top: The first Poseidon MRA1 (P-8A) was delivered to the RAF in October 2019. This was the first of nine such aircraft ordered at a cost of around £3 billion. Above: Poseidon MRA1 lands after a delivery flight to the UK. This page: The first practical mission of the Poseidon MRA1 occurred on 7 August 2020 when an aircraft, accompanied by an RAF Typhoon FGR4, shadowed a Russian warship in the international waters of the North Sea. MoD/Crown Copyright

The first of six P-8A ordered for the RAF was delivered by Boeing in the first week of November 2019. As the aircraft were purchased through the United States Foreign Military sales program, the aircraft had been delivered to the United States Navy at Boeings Tukwila, Washington facility on 29 October that year, before being flown to Naval Air Station Jacksonville for RAF aircrew training prior to delivery to the UK in early 2020 (Boeing & PR, 11.11.2020). The peacetime mission debut for the Poseidon MRA1 took place on 7 August 2020, more than ten years after Britain had relinquished her dedicated maritime patrol capability. During this flight, the Poseidon MRA1 shadowed a Russian warship transiting international waters of the North Sea.

4

POSTSCRIPT

From a heritage perspective the demise of the Nimrod was a severing of Britain's last operational link to her first four engine long range aircraft design of the jet era – the de Havilland Comet passenger transport, from which the Nimrod had been derived.

It is ironic that the fate that befell the Nimrod MRA4 ultimately benefitted the US aerospace/defence industry, as had been the case with the ill-fated Nimrod Airborne Early Warning MK.3 almost a quarter of a century prior. With the demise of the Nimrod MRA4, the British aviation industry would be relegated to minority partner and or basic customer status in regard to large multi-engine jet powered aircraft design and manufacture – an area of expertise that may never be regained as the decline of Britain as a major aerospace design and manufacturing base continues in the twenty first century.

GLOSSARY

AAA	Ageing Aircraft Audit
AEW	Airborne Early Warning
AGM	Air to Ground (surface) Missile
ALARM	Air Launched Anti-Radiation Missile
APU	Auxiliary Power Unit
ASR	Air Staff Requirement
ASRAAM	Advanced Short Range Air to Air Missile
BAe	British Aerospace
BAE	British Aerospace
C^3I	Command Control Communications and Intelligence
cm	Centimetre
COTS	Commercial Off The Shelf
EAC	Equipment Approval Committee
EC	Environmental Control
ECS	Environmental Control System
ELINT	Electronic Intelligence
FCS	Flight Control System
ft.	Foot (feet) – unit of measurement
ft^2.	Foot (feet) squared
GPS	Global Positioning System
IIR	Imaging Infrared
INS	Inertial Navigation System
IOC	Initial Operational Capability
ISTA	Intelligence Surveillance Target Acquisition and Reconnaissance
kg	Kilogram
km	Kilometre(s)
km/h	Kilometres per hour
Knot(s)	Nautical Miles per Hour
KUR	Key User Requirements
lb.	Pound – unit of weight
m	Metre(s)
m^2	Metre(s) squared
MAD	Magnetic Anomaly Detector
MMA	Multi Mission Aircraft
MoD	Ministry of Defence
mph	Miles per hour
MPR	Major Programs Report
MR	Maritime Reconnaissance
MRA	Maritime Reconnaissance Attack
NAO	National Audit Office
NATO	North Atlantic Treaty Organisation
nm	Nautical miles
NR	Nimrod Review

PPR	Publications Parliamentary Records
R	Reconnaissance
RAF	Royal Air Force
RMPA	Replacement Maritime Patrol Aircraft
RR	Rolls Royce
SFC	Specific Fuel Consumption
SLAM ER	Stand-Off Land Attack Missile Enhanced Response
SRLE	Sting Ray Life Extension
SSBN	Nuclear Powered Ballistic Missile Submarine
UK	United Kingdom
USN	United States Navy

BIBLIOGRAPHY

BAE Systems (2002) 'Nimrod MRA4', BAE Systems, Warton, United Kingdom
BAE Systems (2002) 'Nimrod MRA4, The Mighty Hunter', BAE Systems, Warton, United Kingdom
BAE Systems (2004) 'Nimrod MRA4', BAE Systems, Warton, United Kingdom
BAE Systems (2011) *Sting Ray Mod 1 Advanced Lightweight Torpedo*, BAE Systems Maritime Services, United Kingdom
BAE Systems (2018) *Sting Ray Mod 1 Advanced Lightweight Torpedo*, BAE Systems Maritime Services, United Kingdom
Boeing (2019) *Boeing delivers first P-8A Poseidon to United Kingdom's Royal Air Force*, The Boeing Company, USA
Boeing (2020) *AGM/RGM/UGM-84 Harpoon Missile*, The Boeing Company, St Louis, USA
Boeing (undated) *Harpoon Block II, Protecting the Fleet from Sea, Land or Air*, The Boeing Company, St Louis, USA
Carter, M. & Wilson, P. (2000) 'Nimrod MRA4 - The Mighty Hunter', Nimrod Test and Evaluation IPT, BAE Systems, United Kingdom
Gill, A. & Bellamy, A. (2005) 'Flight Testing the Nimrod MRA4', Flight Test (W427E) BAE Systems, Warton, United Kingdom
Haddon-Cave, C. QC (2009) 'The Nimrod Review', Controller of Her Majesty's Stationary Office, Crown Copyright
Harkins, H. (2013) 'Tornado F.2/F.3 Air Defence Variant', Centurion Publishing, United Kingdom
Harkins, H. (2013) 'Eurofighter Typhoon, Storm over Europe', Centurion Publishing, United Kingdom
Harkins, H. (Shannon, C) (2005) 'Royal Air Force Combat Aircraft & Air Launched Weapons, 2005, Centurion Publishing, United Kingdom
Harkins, H. (2010), *letter to Gov.*, Harkins personal correspondence to H.M. Government, United Kingdom
H.M. Government (2010) *Securing Britain in an Age of Uncertainty*: The Strategic Defence and Security Review, HM Government, October 2010
MBDA (2018) *ASRAAM, Within Visual Range Air Dominance Weapon*, Product characteristics, MBDA United Kingdom
MBDA (2019) *Storm Shadow SCALP: Conventionally Armed Long Range Deep Strike Weapon*, MBDA Missile Systems, United Kingdom
Ministry of Defence (1997) 'Major Projects Report 1997', Controller and Auditor General, National Audit Office, House of Commons, United Kingdom Parliament
Ministry of Defence (1999) 'Major Projects Report 1999', Controller and Auditor General, National Audit Office, House of Commons, United Kingdom Parliament
Ministry of Defence (2000) 'Major Projects Report 2000', Controller and Auditor General, National Audit Office, House of Commons, United Kingdom Parliament
Ministry of Defence (2001) 'Major Projects Report 2001', Controller and Auditor General, National Audit Office, House of Commons, United Kingdom Parliament
Ministry of Defence (2002) 'Major Projects Report 2002', Controller and Auditor General, National Audit Office, House of Commons, United Kingdom Parliament
Ministry of Defence (2003) 'Major Projects Report 2003', Controller and Auditor General, National Audit Office, House of Commons, United Kingdom Parliament
Ministry of Defence (2004) 'Major Projects Report 2004', Controller and Auditor General,

National Audit Office, House of Commons, United Kingdom Parliament

Ministry of Defence (2004) 'Major Projects Report 2004: *Project Summary Sheets*, Controller and Auditor General, National Audit Office, House of Commons, United Kingdom Parliament

Ministry of Defence (2005) 'Major Projects Report 2005', Controller and Auditor General, National Audit Office, House of Commons, United Kingdom Parliament

Ministry of Defence (2005) 'Major Projects Report 2005', Controller and Auditor General, National Audit Office, House of Commons, United Kingdom Parliament

Ministry of Defence (2006) 'Major Projects Report 2006', Controller and Auditor General, National Audit Office, House of Commons, United Kingdom Parliament

Ministry of Defence (2007) 'Major Projects Report 2007', Controller and Auditor General, National Audit Office, House of Commons, United Kingdom Parliament

Ministry of Defence (2007) 'Major Projects Report 2007: *Volume II*, Controller and Auditor General, National Audit Office, House of Commons, United Kingdom Parliament

Ministry of Defence (2008) 'Major Projects Report 2008', Controller and Auditor General, National Audit Office, House of Commons, United Kingdom Parliament

Ministry of Defence (2008) 'Major Projects Report 2008', Controller and Auditor General, National Audit Office, House of Commons, United Kingdom Parliament

Ministry of Defence (2009) 'Major Projects Report 2009', Controller and Auditor General, National Audit Office, House of Commons, United Kingdom Parliament

Ministry of Defence (2009) 'Major Projects Report 2009', Controller and Auditor General, National Audit Office, House of Commons, United Kingdom Parliament

Ministry of Defence (2010) 'Major Projects Report 2010', Controller and Auditor General, National Audit Office, House of Commons, United Kingdom Parliament

Ministry of Defence (2011) 'Major Projects Report 2011', Controller and Auditor General, National Audit Office, House of Commons, United Kingdom Parliament

MoD RAF (2004) *ASRAAM, Nothing Comes Close*, Information Sheet, Ministry of Defence, Whitehall, London

Publications, Parliament (2010) *Written Answers for 16 June 2010 – RAF Kinloss*, Publications, Parliament, United Kingdom

Publications, Parliament (2010) *House of Lords data for 16 June 2010 – Nimrod Aircraft*, Publications, Parliament, United Kingdom

Publications, Parliament (2012) *Defence Committee – Future Maritime Surveillance Written Evidence from Dr. Sue Robertson*, Publications, Parliament, United Kingdom

Publications, Parliament (2003) *Nimrod Maritime Reconnaissance Aircraft 4 – Annex A*, Select Committee on Defence Written Evidence, 23 July 2003, Publications, Parliament, United Kingdom

Publications, Parliament (2011) *The Strategic Defence and Security Review and the National Security Strategy – Defence Committee*, Written Evidence, 3 August 2011, Publications, Parliament, United Kingdom

Publications, Parliament (2011) *The Strategic Defence and Security Review and the National Security Strategy*, Written Evidence from Dr. Sue Roberson, 14 March 2011, Publications, Parliament, United Kingdom

Rolls Royce (2020) *BR710 [Product Sheet]*, Rolls Royce

Thales Airborne Systems (2001) *Searchwater 2000AEW*, Thales Sensors, United Kingdom

ABOUT THE AUTHOR

Hugh Harkins FRAS, MIstP, MRAeS is a physicist/historian and author with an extensive research/study background in aeronautic, astronautic, astrophysics, geophysics, nautical and the wider scientific, technical and historical fields. He is also involved in research in the field of Scottish history, which formed a significant element of dual undergraduate degrees. Hugh has published in excess of seventy books, non-fiction and fiction, writing under his given name as well as utilising several pseudonyms. He has also written for several international magazines, whilst his work has been used as reference for many other projects, ranging from the aviation industry, international news corporations and film media to encyclopaedias, museum exhibits and the computer gaming industry. Hugh is an elected Fellow of the Royal Astronomical Society and is an elected member of the Institute of Physics and Royal Aeronautical Society. He currently resides in his native Scotland. Other titles by the author include:

Russian/Soviet Aircraft Carrier & Carrier Aviation Design & Evolution Volume 1 - Seaplane Carriers, Project 71/72, Graf Zeppelin, Project 1123 ASW Cruiser & Project 1143-1143.4 Heavy Aircraft Carrying Cruiser
Soviet Mixed Power Experimental Fighter Aircraft – Piston-Liquid Propellant Rocket Engine/Piston-Ramjet/Piston-Pulsejet & Piston-Compressor Jet Engine Designs of the 1940's
Raid on the Forth - The First German Air Raid on Great Britain in World War II
Light Battle Cruisers and the Second Battle of Heligoland Bight
Russia's Coastal Missile Shield - Bal-E & Bastion Mobile Coastal Cruise Missile Complexes
Iskander - Mobile Tactical Aero-Ballistic/Cruise Missile Complex
Orbital/Fractional Orbit Bombardment System - The Soviet Globalnaya Raketa
Counter-Space Defence Co-Orbital Satellite Fighter
Russia's Strategic Missile Carrier/Bomber Roadmap 2018-2040 – PAK DA, Tu-160M2, Tu-95MSM & Tu-22M3M
Sukhoi T-50/PAK FA - Russia's 5th Generation 'Stealth' Fighter
Sukhoi Su-35S 'Flanker' E - Russia's 4++ Generation Super-Manoeuvrability Fighter
Sukhoi Su-30MKK/MK2/M2 - Russo Kitashiy Striker from Amur
MiG-35/D 'Fulcrum' F – Towards the Fifth Generation
Air War over Syria, Tu-160, Tu-95MS & Tu-22M3 - Cruise Missile and Bombing Strikes on Syria, November 2015-February 2016
Sukhoi Su-27SM(3)/SKM
X-35 – Progenitor to the F-35 Lightning II
X-32 - The Boeing Joint Strike Fighter
Boeing X-36 Tailless Agility Flight Research Aircraft
XF-103 – Mach 3 Stratospheric Interceptor Concept
North American F-108 Rapier - Mach 3 Interceptor
Convair YB-60 - Fort Worth Overcast
Into The Cauldron - The Lancaster MK.I Daylight Raid on Augsburg
Hurricane IIB Combat Log - 151 Wing RAF, North Russia 1941
RAF Meteor Jet Fighters in World War II, an Operational Log
Typhoon IA/B Combat Log - Operation Jubilee, August 1942
Defiant MK.I Combat Log - Fighter Command, May-September 1940
Blenheim MK.IF Combat Log - Fighter Command Day Fighter Sweeps/Night Interceptions, September 1939 - June 1940
Fortress MK.I Combat Log - Bomber Command High Altitude Bombing Operations, July-September1941

www.ingramcontent.com/pod-product-compliance
Lightning Source LLC
Chambersburg PA
CBHW041540220426
43663CB00003B/85